ART TREASURES
AND MUSEUMS
IN AND AROUND
PRESCOTT, ARIZONA

Courthouse Plaza in winter.

ART TREASURES AND MUSEUMS
IN AND AROUND
PRESCOTT, ARIZONA

**Sculptures and Paintings
Histories and Biographies
Historic Buildings, Victorian Homes and Cemeteries
Fine Art Foundries
One- and Two-Day Excursions
Vintage Trains and Aircraft**

Marguerite Madison Aronowitz

**Pine Castle Books
P.O. Box 4397
Prescott, Arizona 86302-4397**

Although the author has made every effort to ensure the accuracy and completeness of information contained in this book, no responsibility is assumed for errors, inaccuracies, omissions, or inconsistencies herein. Any slights of people, places or organizations are unintentional.

Publisher's Cataloging-in-Publication
(Provided by Quality Books, Inc.)

Aronowitz, Marguerite Madison, 1938-
   Art treasures and museums in and around
Prescott, Arizona : sculptures and paintings, histories
and biographies, historic buildings, Victorian homes
and cemeteries, fine art foundries, one- and two-day
excursions, vintage trains and aircraft / Marguerite
Madison Aronowitz. – 1st ed.
   p.cm.
Includes bibliographical references and index.
Library of Congress Control Number: 2001130058
ISBN: 0-9666615-1-6

   1. Art museums—Prescott (Ariz.)—Guidebooks.
2. Art—Prescott (Ariz.)—Guidebooks. 3. Historic
sites—Prescott (Ariz.)—Guidebooks. 4. Historic
buildings—Prescott (Ariz.)—Guidebooks.
5. Prescott (Ariz.)—Guidebooks. I. Title.

N714.P63A76 2001   708.191'57
                                     QBI01-200251

Published by: Pine Castle Books
                  P.O. Box 4397
                  Prescott, AZ 86302-4397

Cover photo: *Early Settlers* by Bill Nebeker, C.A.A.

Printed in the United States of America

Introduction

Prescott, Arizona, is a charming city that houses a vast array of artistic and historic treasures. Over 500 buildings in this scenic area are listed on the National Register of Historic Places, some of which are listed in the chapter featuring the history of Prescott. From picturesque Courthouse Plaza to the sculpture garden of Yavapai College, impressive works of art await your visit. Museums containing historical structures and troves of artifacts offer hours of education and enjoyment.

Among the greatest treasures to come out of Prescott and northern Arizona are people like Buckey O'Neill and Sharlot Hall. Their talent and sacrifices helped make Arizona what it is today. The *Histories and Biographies* section of this book will introduce you to these two fine people, along with artists Solon Borglum, Mary Jane Colter, Kate Cory, Paul Coze and George Phippen. It will also give you a brief history of Fine Art Metal Casting, Fort Whipple, the City of Prescott, and the Yavapai-Prescott Native American Indians.

The large bronze statues to be seen in downtown Prescott were cast in several locations including New York City, but fine art foundries are in fact abundant in the Prescott area. This book will give you a brief history of metal casting and explain the different steps needed to produce a beautiful metal sculpture.

Art and history also abound in nearby locations such as Prescott Valley and Chino Valley. If you have time to venture a little farther out, one- and two-day adventures offer an excuse to spend the day or stay overnight in order to fully appreciate such cities as Flagstaff and Sedona, and such scenic wonders as the Grand Canyon and the Petrified Forest. *Art Treasures and Museums In and Around Prescott, Arizona*, will help you in your search for the beauty, art and history that so enrich Prescott and northern Arizona.

Table of Contents

Note:

Effective June 28, 2001, the **520** Area Code
in northern Arizona will be changed to **928**.

List of Photographs

Prescott Area
Location Addresses

1 Embry-Riddle Aero. Univ.
3200 Willow Creek Road

2 First Congregational Church
216 East Gurley Street

3 Forest Villas Hotel
3645 Lee Circle

4 Fort Whipple Interpretive Ctr
No. Ariz. VA Healthcare Sys
500 North Highway 69

5 Frontier Village Shopping Center
1841 East Highway 69

6 Hassayampa Inn
122 East Gurley Street

7 Heritage Park Zoo
1403 Heritage Park Road

8 Hotel St. Michael
205 West Gurley Street

9 Palace Restaurant and Saloon
120 South Montezuma Street

10 Phippen Museum
4701 North Highway 89

11 Prescott City Hall
201 South Cortez

12 Prescott College
228 Grove Avenue

13 Prescott Courthouse
Courthouse Plaza

14 Prescott Fine Arts Association
208 North Marina Street

15 Prescott Public Library
215 East Goodwin

16 Prescott Resort
1500 Highway 69

17 Prescott Valley Civic Center
7501 Civic Circle North
Prescott Valley

18 Ramada Resort and Spa
4499 East Highway 69

19 Sharlot Hall Museum
415 West Gurley Street

20 Smoki Museum
147 North Arizona Street

21 Stricklin Park
Thumb Butte Rd and Sherwood

22 Wells Fargo Bank
Frontier Village Shopping Center

23 Yavapai College
1100 East Sheldon Street

24 Yavapai Regional Medical Center
1003 Willow Creek Road

Prescott Area
Locations Map

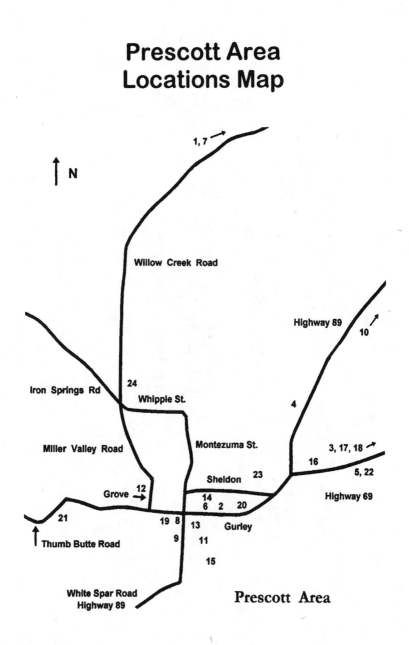

N

1, 7

Willow Creek Road

Highway 89

10

24

Iron Springs Rd

Whipple St.

4

Miller Valley Road

Montezuma St.

3, 17, 18

16

5, 22

Sheldon 23

12

Grove

14

6 2 20

Highway 69

21

19 8

13

Gurley

Thumb Butte Road

9

11

15

White Spar Road
Highway 89

Prescott Area

1. Sculptures

Bronze and other metal sculptures can be found in many locations in the Prescott area. Four major pieces are in or adjacent to Courthouse Plaza; others are nearby. The following sculptures are presented by artist and title:

Solon Borglum	*Cowboy at Rest*
	Solon Borglum Bronze Collection
	William O'Neill Rough Rider
	Monument
Kit Carson	*Big Dukie*
Rebecca Davis and	*Permian Corridor*
Roger Asay	*Robert Sullivan Memorial*
	Stone Circle, Butte Creek
John L. Dobberteen	*Arizona Moon*
	Eagle
	Iron Tree
	Untitled piece
R. Einfrank	Untitled piece
GABALDON	*Ceremonial Trophy* (page 20)
Cari Gail	*Proud Heritage of the Indian*
Ralph Hartleigh	*Lost Rainbow* (page 20)
Heath Krieger	*Sphinx Recumbent*
Natalie Krol	*Silver Tornado*
Neil Logan	*All Veterans Memorial*
Richard Marcusen	*Community Gothic*
Patricia Mathiesen	*Spirit of the Frontier*
	Viola
Tom McClure	*Helix*
Lanét Moravec	*Identity Emerging*
Bill Nebeker, C.A.A.	*Early Settlers*
John Skurja	*Leaps and Bounds*
Richard Terry	*Early Rodeo*
Michael Tierney	*Limitless*
Dr. Lloyd Wadleigh	*The Eagles*
Lyman Whittaker	*Double Helix Horizontal*
unknown artist	*Homage to Viola Jimulla*

Art Treasures and Museums In and Around Prescott, Arizona

By location:

Downtown

City Hall
Early Rodeo

Courthouse Plaza
All Veterans Memorial
Cowboy at Rest
William O'Neill Rough Rider Monument

Metropolitan Prescott

Embry-Riddle Aeronautical University
Eagle
The Eagles

Frontier Village
Spirit of the Frontier

Intersection of Highways 69 and 89
Early Settlers

Prescott Fine Arts Association
Sphinx Recumbent

Prescott Resort
Proud Heritage of the Indian
Viola

Stricklin Park
Stone Circle and Robert Sullivan Memorial

Yavapai College
Arizona Moon
Big Dukie
Community Gothic
Double Helix Horizontal
Helix
Homage to Viola Jimulla
Identity Emerging
Iron Tree, Lost Rainbow and Ceremonial Trophy
Leaps and Bounds
Permian Corridor
Untitled (2)

Yavapai Regional Medical Center
Silver Tornado

Prescott Valley Civic Center

Limitless
Solon Borglum Bronze Collection

Fine art is that in which the hand,
the head and the heart go together.
(John Ruskin, *The Two Paths,*
Lecture ii.)

THE SCULPTURES

Cowboy at Rest is a rather recent addition to Courthouse Plaza, having been dedicated in 1990. This large and impressive bronze was "pointed up" or enlarged from a Solon Borglum miniature, with the approval of the Borglum family. It was commissioned by the Prescott Community Art Trust, headed by former Prescott mayor Jerri Wagner, and cast at Skurja Art Castings in Prescott.

Cowboy at Rest was sculpted prior to the 1904 Louisiana Purchase Exposition that was held in St. Louis, Missouri (St. Louis World's Fair). It was entitled *The Lookout* and was described as portraying life on the prairie with mystery, silence and atmosphere.

The magnificent bronze *Sioux Indian Buffalo Dancer* is but one of the 27 Borglum bronze miniatures on temporary display at the Prescott Valley Civic Center. One day the Prescott Community Art Trust, who owns these pieces, hopes to establish a museum that will house these treasures and pay tribute to the artistic genius of Solon Borglum. Inquire at the Department of Public Works desk for an exhibit guide to the Borglum bronzes.

Solon Borglum's *William O'Neill Rough Rider Monument* portrays one of Prescott's most famous sons, Buckey O'Neill, who led a local contingent of men to war in 1898. As the soldiers walked to the Prescott train depot followed by their wives and sweethearts, they were about to join the many men from the West and Southwest who had volunteered to fight in the Spanish-American War. The Rough Riders played an important part in Teddy Roosevelt's assault on Kettle Hill and San Juan Hill in 1898. Captain William "Buckey" O'Neill was killed just prior to the attack on Kettle Hill. O'Neill is featured in the *Histories and Biographies* section of this book

This beautiful bronze was sculpted in Connecticut, cast in New York, and traveled by train to Prescott, where it arrived the same day the dedication celebration was scheduled, July 3, 1907. The dedication was attended by Maurice O'Neill, Buckey's adopted son.

4

Recently restored, this famous figure epitomizes the spirit of the West and the brave men and women who defined Prescott in its early days. The large, 28-ton granite boulder on which it is mounted was taken from a local mountain. This extraordinary sculpture is considered to be one of the finest equestrian statues in the world.

When Solon Borglum was asked to create a fitting monument to Buckey O'Neill and the Rough Riders, he agreed even though the $10,000 raised by local adults and school children was far less than his normal fee. This work is considered to be one of Borglum's finest sculptures.

THE ARTIST

Further information on Solon Borglum can be found in the *Histories and Biographies* section.

COWBOY AT REST

SCULPTOR: Solon Borglum cast the miniature

LOCATION: Courthouse Square, Downtown Prescott

SOLON BORGLUM
BRONZE COLLECTION

SCULPTOR: Solon H. Borglum

LOCATION: Prescott Valley Civic Center

Sioux Indian Buffalo Dancer (1903).

Two of 27 Borglum bronzes on display in Prescott
Valley Civic Center. Left: *The Indian Love Chase* (1899);
right: *Bear Looking Down* (1897).

WILLIAM O'NEILL
ROUGH RIDER MONUMENT

SCULPTOR: Solon H. Borglum

LOCATION: Courthouse Square, Downtown Prescott

(Pamela DeMarais)

THE SCULPTURE

This imposing sculpture stands high and dramatic atop the Quad between Yavapai College's bookstore and library. Constructed from telephone poles, rock boulders, steel and chains, it was installed by the artist in 1973. The poles are imbedded 6 feet into the ground. In the '70s the Quad was nicknamed the "prison yard" and Carson wanted his sculpture to reflect the architecture of the utilitarian buildings and add warmth by incorporating natural elements. He first created a jewelry-scale model using balsa and clay, then scaled it up to its gigantic proportions. Using a chain saw and eventually crane and tow truck, he put it in place. The name "Big Dukie" comes from the name of a fellow artist named Dukie who autographed the top of one of the poles with a chain saw.

THE ARTIST

Kit Carson lives in New River, Arizona He has been creating hand-engraved jewelry for 25 years and maintains his studio there. He continues to sculpt from rusty recycled steel he has found on his Route 66 travels. He has shows around the country, most recently in New York, Santa Fe, England and Ireland. Kit can be reached at Cactus Camp, 45635 North 20th Street, New River, Arizona 85087. Telephone/fax 623/465-2680.

BIG DUKIE

SCULPTOR: Kit Carson

LOCATION: Yavapai College Upper Quad

(Pamela DeMarais)

THE SCULPTURES

Permian Corridor is an unusual contemporary sculpture created from Arizona flagstone slabs, roughly two inches thick, arranged vertically in two rows planted directly into the surrounding decomposed granite. The newest addition to Yavapai College's Sculpture Garden, *Permian Corridor* interacts with light and shade, changing with the time of day and season. The artists use nature's raw materials to create art that presents a direct and pure visual experience. They have combined straight-cut and ragged edges to produce energetic contrast. The viewer is invited to examine the minute variations of color and surface that appear not only here but throughout nature.

Stone Circle, Butte Creek and the *Robert Sullivan Memorial* are located in Prescott's small but charming Stricklin Park. *Stone Circle* is composed of lichen-covered stones that create an enclosed space with a strong presence that seems to have existed there from early times. This sculpture carries on a dialogue with the *Robert Sullivan Memorial*: two lines of boulders converging at right angles and rising to a corner. One of the corner stones serves as a bench. The placement of stones suggests an ancient ruin.

THE ARTISTS

Having lived in Colorado and New Mexico, Rebecca Davis and Roger Asay moved to Prescott in 1982. Shortly afterward they began their collaboration in producing sculpture that has been shown in museums throughout the West. They have created large public sculptures that can be seen in Tucson, Cottonwood, and Phoenix, and can be reached at (520)778-7481. Their mailing address is 1542 Shoup Street, Prescott 86305; sky@goodnet.com; www.goodnet.com/~skye.

PERMIAN CORRIDOR

SCULPTORS: Rebecca Davis and Roger Asay

LOCATION: Yavapai College Sculpture Garden

ROBERT SULLIVAN MEMORIAL

SCULPTORS: Rebecca Davis and Roger Asay

LOCATION: Stricklin Park

STONE CIRCLE, BUTTE CREEK

SCULPTORS: Rebecca Davis and Roger Asay

LOCATION: Stricklin Park

(Roger Asay)

THE SCULPTURE

Arizona Moon is a welded steel piece that greets students and visitors alike who drive into the main entrance of Yavapai College. It was created and installed in the early 1980s.

THE ARTIST

John L. Dobberteen, who died in 1987, was originally from Michigan. A man of many interests and talents, he moved to Arizona in 1973 although he continued to fly out of Los Angeles until 1975 as a pilot for TWA. As an artist John participated in metal sculpture classes at Yavapai College, where he created several large pieces that can be seen in the Prescott area today. He was president of the Mountain Artists Guild and a member of several fraternal organizations including the Silver Eagles of Embry-Riddle Aeronautical University.

ARIZONA MOON

SCULPTOR: John L. Dobberteen

LOCATION: Entrance to Yavapai College

(Pamela DeMarais)

EAGLE

SCULPTOR: Captain John L. Dobberteen

LOCATION: Embry-Riddle Aeronautical University
between Buildings 17 and 19

(Pamela DeMarais)

THE SCULPTURES

Three sculptures are included in the following grouping. From left to right they are *Iron Tree* by John L. Dobberteen, *Lost Rainbow* by Ralph Hartleigh (also see inset), and *Ceremonial Trophy* by GABALDON.

Iron Tree was fabricated from sheet steel, *Rainbow* from sheet steel and bronze, and *Ceremonial Trophy* from steel and telephone poles. They were installed in 1982, 1979-80, and 1976, respectively. All three sculptures were created in Charles Clements' art and architecture workshops.

THE ARTISTS

Iron Tree is the third of four sculptures in this book by John Dobberteen (see page 16).

Lost Rainbow is by Ralph Hartleigh, who today works as a sculptor and foundry man in Camp Verde, Arizona. A native of the state, he enjoyed art as a child and pursued his dreams of working as an artist even though he spent several years in the U.S. Air Force and additional time in the U.S. Forest Service as a firefighter. After completing art courses at Yavapai College, where he received a commission to design and build *Lost Rainbow*, he opened his own studio. His custom sculpture, which he takes from mold to patina, is shown at exhibits nationwide. He can be reached at his studio, (520)567-5107, where he is happy to greet visitors. Please call ahead to set up an appointment. His work can also be see in the A'Loft Gallery in Bashford Courts, downtown Prescott. Hartleigh's website is hartleighart@wildapache.net.

GABALDON, who designed/constructed *Ceremonial Trophy* in 1976, works as a designer/builder/educator on his ranch in Arizona. Commission work to P.O. Box 44306, Tucson, AZ 85733.

IRON TREE, LOST RAINBOW, AND CEREMONIAL TROPHY

SCULPTORS: John L. Dobberteen, Ralph Hartleigh and GABALDON

LOCATION: Yavapai College Upper Quad

(Pamela DeMarais)

UNTITLED

SCULPTOR: John L. Dobberteen

LOCATION: Yavapai College between Buildings 5 and 7

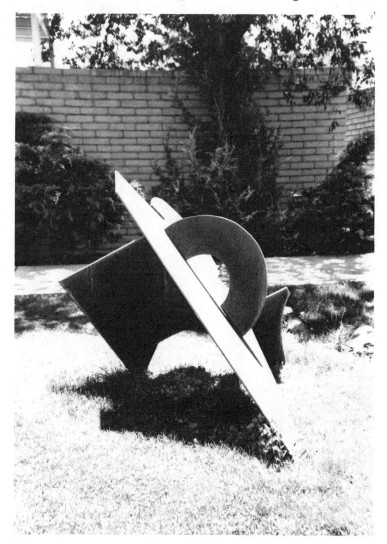

THE SCULPTURE

This modern sculpture mounted upon the side of Building 4 is constructed from wood and found metal objects. It was created during Charles Clements' art and architecture workshops in the 1970s. Students were chosen for the workshops through faculty recommendations, and each sculpture was created for a specifically selected site, both on- and off-campus. Models were made and accepted sculptures were made full-size and installed by the students.

THE ARTIST

R. Einfrank could not be located.

UNTITLED

SCULPTOR: R. Einfrank

LOCATION: Yavapai College Upper Quad

THE SCULPTURE

Proud Heritage of the Indian sits majestically at the entrance to the Prescott Resort, Dedicated in 1992, this large bronze was commissioned by the Prescott Community Art Trust and cast at Skurja Art Castings in Prescott.

THE ARTIST

Cari Gail could not be located.

PROUD HERITAGE
OF THE INDIAN

SCULPTOR: Cari Gail

LOCATION: Entrance of the Prescott Resort

THE SCULPTURE

Sphinx Recumbent is a sleek bronze that was cast at Skurja Art Castings in Prescott. It is one of a six-piece edition, and was installed on North Marina in the mid-1980s. Located next to the Prescott Fine Arts Association offices in a small courtyard, *Sphinx* invites one to stop and take a moment to relax during a busy day. The name of the sculpture was taken from the book *Raintree County*.

One might also pause to reflect on the PFAA theater which is housed in a 1891 gothic church structure formerly home of the Catholic Church of the Sacred Heart of Jesus. More information about the buildings is available in the Association offices.

THE ARTIST

Heath Krieger is a Prescott resident artist who has been throwing pots since 1968. He attended the Brooks Institute of Fine Arts in Santa Barbara, California, before pursuing a career in the world of ceramics. Heath has a studio in town where he throws large ceramic vessels, does ceramic sculptures, and creates an occasional metal sculpture.

SPHINX RECUMBENT

SCULPTOR: Heath Krieger

LOCATION: Prescott Fine Arts Association
208 North Marina Street

(Pamela DeMarais)

THE SCULPTURE

Silver Tornado is a tribute to the cattle industry in and around Prescott and is also a symbol of Prescott's famed rodeo. Cast in stainless steel, *Tornado* bucks high in the air and could not be cast from the softer metal, bronze, because of its stance and weight of 4,000 pounds. The animal represented is a Saler bull.

THE ARTIST

Natalie Krol is a local artist who casts bronze and stainless steel sculptures. She also works in copper repoussé (hammered copper as was used in creating the Statue of Liberty). She is renowned for her unusually posed figures such as *Kim, Olympic Rhythms*, which is made of copper repoussé, stands 11 feet high and 9 feet wide, and is balanced on a 4-inch toe section with no visible support. *Kim* is twirling a stainless steel ribbon and today stands gracefully in Brea, California. Natalie pioneered casting fine art in stainless steel, and has sold over 600 artworks to private collectors, plus 30 monumental-sized outdoor public pieces. She is currently working on a commission for a sculpture to be placed in a new Mayo Clinic building in Rochester, Minnesota, and is a partner in the new Jaren-Krol Gallery located at 107 East Willis Street, Prescott. Telephone (520)443-7721.

SILVER TORNADO

SCULPTOR: Natalie Krol

LOCATION: On Whipple Street, in front of
Yavapai Regional Medical Center

(Pamela DeMarais)

THE SCULPTURE

The *All Veterans Memorial* is a tribute to Yavapai County veterans who gave their lives in World War I, World War II, Korea, and Vietnam. It was dedicated in 1989. The American fighting men depicted in this moving bronze are in Vietnam, and the wounded man is being aided by a fellow soldier who is awaiting a medical helicopter. This portrayal of the sorrows of war was created by artist Neil Logan.

THE ARTIST

Neil Logan was born in Prescott and served in Vietnam for 27 months during the conflict. Upon returning home he attended Northern Arizona University in Flagstaff where he received his degree in art. Prescott's *All Veterans Memorial* was Logan's second life-sized veterans sculpture, the first being *Served With Honor* that is located in the courthouse plaza of Longview, Texas. Logan's whereabouts could not be determined at this time.

ALL VETERANS MEMORIAL

SCULPTOR: Neil Logan

LOCATION: Courthouse Square, Downtown Prescott

THE SCULPTURE

This striking sculpture was commissioned by the Friends of Yavapai College Art in 1985 and completed in 1986-87. It was installed in the Sculpture Garden in 1998, after having been first placed on the corner of Rush and Sheldon, followed by a brief period in front of the Yavapai College Gallery. Constructed of mild steel tubing and sheet metal, it is welded and painted. *Community Gothic* is an outstanding example of Professor Marcusen's expression of spatial relationships integrated with his exploration of tall, vertical abstracted stylizations of the human figure. He is a student of Cubistic reassociation and segmentation of sculptural space, in the style of Pablo Picasso and Paul Cezanne. This form of art lends itself to the use of many types of metal that initially resists change but in the hands of a master can be shaped and molded.

THE ARTIST

Richard Marcusen is a retired art Professor from the Yavapai College Fine Arts Department who taught sculpture, jewelry and woodworking for many years. He holds an undergraduate degree in Painting from Brigham Young University and a Masters in Jewelry and Sculpture from the University of Oregon. He has taken postgraduate work at the University of Copenhagen, the Tyler School of Art, and Arizona State University. A distinguished member of Prescott's art community, Professor Marcusen taught art from 1963-2000 in California and Arizona, retiring from teaching in May 2000.

COMMUNITY GOTHIC

SCULPTOR: Richard Marcusen

LOCATION: Yavapai College Sculpture Garden

(Pamela DeMarais)

THE SCULPTURES

Spirit of the Frontier depicts two women, a baby and a young boy as they might have appeared in the early days of Prescott, when wives and mothers struggled to keep their families alive and well. Regardless of whether you were a Native American or a homesteader from the East, the hardships were the same.

Viola, the beautifully detailed bronze in the lobby of the Prescott Resort, depicts Viola Jimulla, who was Chieftess of the Yavapai Tribe from 1940 until she died in 1966. An expert basket maker, Viola is accompanied by her granddaughter, Pat McGee, who is the young girl. (See *Histories and Biographies* section, *The Yavapai-Prescott Native American Indians.*)

THE ARTIST

Pat Mathiesen, sculptor and painter, works today from her studio in Bozeman, Montana. After having lived in the Pacific Northwest, Alaska, California and Arizona, she is drawn to the simpler themes of the past as she paints the pristine beauty of the Montana mountains, the rural wheat fields and country roads, and ever-captivating horses. A largely self-taught sculptor, Pat has executed life-sized or larger sculptures that can be seen in Scottsdale, Phoenix and Prescott, Arizona; Milwaukee, Wisconsin; Chicago, Illinois; and Bozeman, Montana. Her work is also part of the private collections of the New York Life Insurance Co., the American Quarter Horse Association, the Trammel Crow Company, and the William Grace Company, among others. She has participated in many invitational shows, including the Tucson Museum of Art and Mesa Southwest Museum in Arizona, and the National Cowboy Hall of Fame Museum in Oklahoma City. Her work has been published in *Southwest Art Magazine, Arizona Highways, Contemporary Western Artists,* and *Contemporary Women Sculptors.* She can be reached at 3480 Sunflower Road, Bozeman, MT 59715. Telephone (406)585-8550.

SPIRIT OF THE FRONTIER

SCULPTOR: Pat Mathiesen

LOCATION: In front of the Frontier Village Shopping Center

VIOLA

SCULPTOR: Pat Mathiesen

LOCATION: Prescott Resort

(Pamela DeMarais)

Sculpture is more divine, and more
  like Nature,
That fashions all her works in high relief,
And that is sculpture. This vast ball, the
  Earth,
Was moulded out of clay, and baked in
  fire;
Men, women, and all animals that breathe
Are statues and not paintings.
(Longfellow, *Michael Angelo*. Pt. iii, sec. 5)

THE SCULPTURE

Helix is fabricated from welded aluminum sheet. It was created in 1975 and installed in the Sculpture Garden in 1999. This fine piece is part of a grouping of 10 sculptures that were designed as an environmental grouping big enough to walk in and through. Other pieces in the grouping are located in Florida, Michigan and Wisconsin.

THE ARTIST

Tom McClure is a Prescott artist who retired from the University of Michigan after teaching for 31 years as a Professor of Art. His work is featured in many galleries around the country, and can be found in numerous public collections from Seattle to Detroit. Educated at the University of Nebraska, Washington State University and Cranbrook Academy of Art where he received his Master's Degree, Mr. McClure also studied in Italy and was employed by Boeing in Seattle for four years during World War II before becoming an art professor at the the School for American Craftsmen at Alfred University in Alfred, New York. After that he taught at the University of Oklahoma in Norman, and the University of Michigan in Ann Arbor. He has won many awards during his lifetime and has commissioned pieces at the Ford Motor Company in Dearborn, Michigan, the University of Michigan in Ann Arbor and Dearborn, and the DeWaters Art Center in Flint, among others. The list of exhibits in which he has shown range from Syracuse and Philadelphia to St. Paul, Minnesota, and Los Angeles. He has also had many one-man exhibits around the country.

HELIX

SCULPTOR: Tom McClure

LOCATION: Yavapai College Sculpture Garden

THE SCULPTURE

Identity Emerging is a four-piece sculpture located on Yavapai College' Upper Quad between Building 2 and the Library. This graceful grouping that abstractly represents people with openness of mind and heart is constructed of cast concrete with mosaics of river stones and crushed brick. The sculptures symbolize humankind's pursuit of life through knowledge, heart, mind, soul, sexuality, and the unique art of being "whoever you are." The sheltering willow tree, which is part of the grouping, is a symbol of humankind's ability to withstand the challenges of life with strength. *Identity Emerging* was created in Yavapai College's art-in-architecture workshops and installed in 1975.

THE ARTIST

Lanét Moravec is a Prescott area artist who was born in South Dakota, where she grew to love the vast space of the Dakota Prairie. It was the influence of nature: the distinct seasons, the bright all-enveloping sun and the pure air that shaped her vision and awakened her desire to express herself through art. She has studied at the University of Maryland, University of Miami, and Yavapai College, is a Phi Theta Kappan, and has lived in 46 different locations during her lifetime. Lanét's art reflects her love of people from all walks of life; all cultures, creeds and races. A mother of three, she continues to study art at Yavapai College as she creates a legacy for her public and her family. She lives in Prescott with her husband, a health care administrator and psychologist, and their youngest daughter.

Lanét fondly remembers being in the late Charles Clements' workshops in the 1970s, where she learned the premise of Clements' belief in "art-in-architecture." Students in the workshop competed for the honor of creating a sculpture that would be installed on the main campus; many of the pieces in place today are a result of these workshops.

IDENTITY EMERGING

SCULPTOR: Lanét Moravec

LOCATION: Yavapai College Upper Quad

THE SCULPTURE

Dedicated in 1985, this impressive bronze was the first statue to be dedicated in Prescott since the *William O'Neill Rough Rider Monument* in 1907. *Early Settlers* represents some of the first people who came to Prescott: mule skinner, gold panner, cowboy, and bonneted woman who holds her bible as she shields her eyes from the bright Arizona sun. When Nebeker first designed the piece, the figures consisted of the three men with the possible addition of a Fort Whipple soldier. After discussing the figures with his wife and father, however, who came from early pioneer heritage, Bill added a pioneer woman. She represents the important role played by women in the early days of the Southwest and the settling of the Arizona Territory. The result is what you see today—the monumental and magnificent bronze *Early Settlers*.

THE ARTIST

Bill Nebeker, C.A.A., was raised on a farm in Idaho until he was ten years old and his family moved to Prescott. As a youngster he showed talent as a whittler who would create small horses and dogs from bits of wood. After attending an art show of sculptures created by master sculptor George Phippen, Bill knew he wanted to pursue sculpting as a career. As a young man he was hired to work in Phippen's bronze factory, where for ten years he learned the trade and studied Phippen's techniques. After fifteen years of sculpting and creating his own bronzes, he was able to present his work in the Cowboy Artists of America Show. Bill's dream had come true, and today he is one of the premier bronze sculptors in the world. He work is displayed in galleries from Scottsdale to Dallas, Santa Fe and Chicago. Two other Nebeker monumental pieces to be found in Arizona are *Territorial Sheriff* in Glendale, and the *Memorial Tribute* to the Arizona Department of Public Safety (ADPS) located on 21st Street and West Encanto Boulevard in Phoenix.

EARLY SETTLERS

SCULPTOR: Bill Nebeker, C.A.A.

LOCATION: Junction of Sheldon and Gurley Streets

THE SCULPTURE

Leaps and Bounds, created by Prescott artist John Skurja, was first cast in 1993. The sculpture exhibited in Yavapai College's Sculpture Garden was cast and installed in 1998. This animated bronze frog immediately catches the viewer's eye as one enters the Garden. It appears to be in motion, ready to escape the confines of the grassy area. Or perhaps it is dancing or jumping with joy.

THE ARTIST

Native Prescottonian John Skurja is well known for his work in metal. He owns and operates Skurja Art Castings, a fine art foundry just off Commerce Drive on Spire Drive (see *Histories and Biographies* under *Fine Art Metal Casting*). After earning his Bachelor's Degree in Art Education at Arizona State University, he obtained his Masters from Northern Arizona University in Flagstaff. He then taught art in the Prescott Public Schools, following which he began casting bronze. Skurja is an accomplished artist in many forms, including his work in jewelry and sculpture. He exhibits regularly at galleries in Arizona, California and Colorado.

Frogs are John's favorite subject. He has studied them extensively and uses his talent to convey a sense of their vulnerability, beauty, and importance in the world. His unusual frog sculpture *Heavy Thoughts* (in the style of Rodin's *The Thinker*) can be seen in Cypress Gardens, Florida, and in the Na Aina Kai Botanical/Sculpture Gardens on the island of Kauai, Hawaii. Skurja can be reached at Skurja Art Castings, 1056 Spire Drive, Prescott. Telephone 520/778-3651.

LEAPS AND BOUNDS

SCULPTOR: John Skurja

LOCATION: Yavapai College Sculpture Garden

THE SCULPTURE

Dedicated in 1988 to celebrate 100 years of rodeo in Prescott, *Early Rodeo* portrays the beauty and excitement of man and horse in rodeo competition. This impressive bronze was cast at Skurja Art Castings in Prescott.

THE ARTIST

Richard (Rick) Terry, who has his studio in Whitehall, Montana, has been an artist practically all his life. As a college student at the Northern Arizona University in Flagstaff in the 1970 he focused on sculpture and bronze casting. In 1979 he went to work for the fine arts foundry Buffalo Bronze Works in Sedona, then in 1986 he was awarded a commission by the Prescott Community Art Trust to create the monumental bronze *Early Rodeo* that we see today in front of Prescott's City Hall. After completing this work he went on to become the assistant to famous Disney sculptor, Blaine Gibson, helping in the creation of several large bronzes, starting with an eight-foot figure of Sam Rayburn for the town of Bonham, Texas, which was unveiled in 1989. In 1993 they created a larger-than-life Walt Disney and Mickey Mouse for California's Disneyland. Additional castings were made for Disney's Magic Kingdom in Florida and the Disney theme park in Tokyo, Japan. To commemorate the end of World War II, Gibson and Terry teamed up again to create an eight-foot bronze of U.S. Marine aviator Joe Foss for Sioux Falls, South Dakota. A life-size bronze of Roy Disney and Minnie Mouse was completed in 1999 and installed at Disney World in Florida. (*Early Rodeo, Sam Rayburn, Joe Foss* and the Disney sculptures were all cast at Skurja Art Castings in Prescott.) Although still working with Blaine Gibson, Rick himself has been commissioned to create numerous pieces depicting historical, wildlife and military subjects. After spending 20 years in the Sedona area, Rick and his wife Lynn have recently relocated to Whitehall, Montana. They can be reached at their ranch: 895 Whitetail Road, Whitehall, Montana 59759.

EARLY RODEO

SCULPTOR: Richard Terry

LOCATION: Prescott City Hall
Cortez and Goodwin Streets

THE SCULPTURE

Limitless is a brightly colored geometric steel sculpture whose cantilevered forms reach skyward from the courtyard of the new Prescott Valley Civic Center Plaza on Lakeshore Drive near Glassford Hill Road. This contemporary piece complements the modern lines of the Civic Center, which will be the centerpiece of the Prescott Valley's exciting new theatre and commercial area. When artist Michael Tierney first visited the area, he was impressed with the city government's open-mindedness and desire to improve and expand the city. With that in mind he set out to create a form that expressed the progressive future of the area. He believes the design of any sculpture should encourage discussion and draw people toward it. *Limitless'* arms were meant to reach skyward and represent the unlimited desire Prescott Valley had to grow and embrace the future. The name of the sculpture came from Tierney's Irish family's philosophy of living life *gan teora*, which means "without limits" or "limitless." He said, "The idea has been with me most of my life, this outlook on life not only fits the philosophy of the City of Prescott Valley, but also follows my own personal ideals. This is why the project holds a very special place in my life."

THE ARTIST

Michael Tierney currently lives in a suburb of Austin, Texas, where he works as an architect designing custom homes, building sculpture, and creating modern furniture. He has a B.A. from Arizona State University and a Masters from Cal Poly Pomona. An expert in geometric design, his favorite media are steel, glass and concrete. He can be reached at 1801 Warner Ranch Road, #222, Round Rock, TX 78664. Telephone 512/828-0545, e-mail mictierney@yahoo.com. or mesomorphic2000@yahoo.com.

LIMITLESS

SCULPTOR: Michael Tierney

LOCATION: Prescott Valley Civic Center Plaza

THE SCULPTURE

The Eagles is a dramatic piece fabricated from copper and steel that towers eight feet high and features two eagles in combat over a lucrative fishing perch. The eagles portrayed are immature bald eagles, and the attacking eagle is especially impressive, especially since it contains 2,000 feathers cut one at a time. The artist worked 20 hours per week for two years to complete this piece.

THE ARTIST

Dr. Lloyd Wadleigh is a Prescott resident who ventured into sculpture and jewelry making after teaching economics and business in California, Ohio and Wisconsin for 36 years. After retiring to Prescott in 1984, he enrolled in jewelry making at Yavapai College, subsequently moving on to sculpture and finally welding where he combined all his skills to create *The Eagles*. This beauty proudly stands on the grounds of Embry-Riddle Aeronautical University in the grassy area near the cafeteria building. At Yavapai College Dr. Wadleigh was instrumental in setting up a course in metal sculpture as art, and was guided through the process of his coursework by Professor Dick Marcusen, whose *Community Gothic* can be seen in the Yavapai College Sculpture Garden. Since completing *The Eagles*, Dr. Wadleigh has continued to work in silver and has designed jewelry featuring attacking eagles.

THE EAGLES

THE ARTIST: Dr. Lloyd Wadleigh

LOCATION: Embry-Riddle Aeronautical University, near the Cafeteria Building

Detail from *The Eagles*
(Pamela DeMarais)

THE SCULPTURE

Double Helix Horizontal is one of the latest additions to Yavapai College's popular Sculpture Garden, having been installed in 2000. A stately, revolving kinetic wind sculpture 19 feet high, it was crafted by artist Lyman Whitaker from stainless steel and patinated copper. It rests on a sealed ball bearing at the top of the vertical rod, allowing it to revolve and undulate in the slightest breeze. The artist combines art, science, and architecture in his work to give the viewer a sense of symmetry and motion that fascinates, calms, and reassures.

THE ARTIST

Lyman Whitaker is a native of Utah, where in 1978 he received his B.F.A. from the University of Utah, Salt Lake City. A sculptor for over 40 years, Whitaker has spent the last 13 years creating wind sculptures that range in size from 5 to 28 feet. His fascinating and elegant creations have been installed in locations from Los Alamos, New Mexico, to Estes Park, Colorado, and Jackson, Michigan. A grouping of 13 were installed at Vermont's Bennington Center for the Arts in 2000. Artist Whitaker and his wife Stacy Christensen reside in the desert southwest with their two young children. His sculptures can be seen in fine art galleries such as the El Prado Gallery in Sedona's Tlaquepaque Arts and Crafts Village. Here can be found a "wind forest" containing over 50 Whitaker sculptures in different sizes and shapes that dance to the rhythms of nature. Contact the El Prado Gallery at P.O. Box 1849, Sedona AZ 86339 for a color brochure. Telephone (800)498-3300; fax 520/282-7578.

DOUBLE HELIX HORIZONTAL

SCULPTOR: Lyman Whitaker

LOCATION: Yavapai College Sculpture Garden

THE SCULPTURE

Homage to Viola Jimulla, Yavapai Chieftess and Basketmaker is fabricated from sheet metal. Located on the north side of Building 1 on the Yavapai College upper Quad, this striking sculpture's straight lines are set off against the plain brick wall. It was created in 1973 by one of the college's art students.

THE ARTIST

Unknown (initials W.P.).

HOMAGE TO VIOLA JIMULLA, YAVAPAI CHIEFTESS AND BASKETMAKER

SCULPTOR: Student

LOCATION: Yavapai College Upper Quad

The moral life of a man forms part of the subject-matter of the artist, but the morality of art consists in the perfect use of an imperfect medium.
(Oscar Wilde, *The Picture of Dorian Gray: Preface*)

2. Paintings

Tucked away in several Prescott area locations are paintings on public display that reflect the history and drama of Prescott and the West. Some display glorious color and others have become a bit faded with time. There are grand murals to be seen and modern depictions of cowboy stars. Many were painted by artists of world renown; others by lesser-known painters. Within this section the following paintings are presented by artist and title:

Hermon Adams	*Cloud Dancer*
	Snow Wolf
	The Challenge
Creston Baumgartner	*Smoki People of Prescott*
Kate J. Cory	*Buffalo Dancer*
	Carding Wool
	Indian Gathering
	Kopi Butterfly
	Migration
	Migration of the Hopi Tribe in the Early 20th Century
	Return of the Kachinas
Paul Coze	Large mural on canvas
	Prelude to Modern Prescott
	William Hickling Prescott
Cheryl Foley	*Tom Mix*
Ronald Hedge	Hassayampa murals
Vincent M. Hovley	Junior Bonner mural
Charles E. Kemp	*Prescott 1900*
Fred Lucas	*Grand Canyon*
	Mustangs
George Molnar	*A Little Girl from Cameron*
	On Top of the World
	Prescott Princess
George Phippen	*The Walker Party*

By location:

Downtown

<u>City Hall</u>
Large mural on canvas by Paul Coze
Smoki People of Prescott by Creston Baumgartner
William Hickling Prescott by Paul Coze
<u>First Congregational Church</u>
*Migration of the Hopi Tribe in the Early 20th
Century* by Kate Cory
<u>Hassayampa Hotel</u>
Wall murals by Ronald Hedge
<u>Palace Restaurant and Saloon</u>
Junior Bonner mural by Vincent Hovley
<u>Smoki Museum</u>
Buffalo Dancer by Kate Cory
Kopi Butterfly by Kate Cory
Migration by Kate Cory
Return of the Kachinas by Kate Cory
<u>Prescott Public Library</u>
Carding Wool by Kate Cory
Indian Gathering by Kate Cory
The Walker Party by George Phippen

Metropolitan Prescott

<u>Phippen Museum</u>
Prelude to Modern Prescott by Paul Coze
<u>Prescott Resort</u>
A Little Girl from Cameron by George Molnar
Cloud Dancer by Hermon Adams
Grand Canyon by Fred Lucas
Mustangs by Fred Lucas
On Top of the World by George Molnar
Prescott Princess by George Molnar
Snow Wolf by Hermon Adams
The Challenge by Hermon Adams
<u>Ramada Resort and Spa</u>
Tom Mix by Cheryl Foley
<u>Wells Fargo Bank</u> (Frontier Village)
Prescott 1900 by Charles Kemp

Art is a human activity having for
its purpose the transmission to
others of the highest and best
feelings to which men have risen.
(Count Leo Tolstoy, *What is Art?*
Chap. viii.)

THE PAINTINGS

Snow Wolf will draw you to the far end of the Prescott Resort's ballroom corridor with its dramatic beauty and depth. Artist Hermon Adams created this painting from inspiration he received from Henry Wadsworth Longfellow's lyric poem *Song of Hiawatha*. The lifelike images of the hunter and wolf fighting the blowing frigid winter reach out from the canvas with intensity. Adams has used *Song of Hiawatha* for 20 years as inspiration for his extraordinary paintings.

Two other oils by artist Adams are also on display in the Prescott Resort. *The Challenge* evokes the spirit of the hunt. *Cloud Dancer* is graceful and powerful, leaping off the canvas as the bronze wing of the eagle reaches out and over the frame—giving the painting three dimensions.

THE ARTIST

Prescott artist Hermon Adams was born and raised in Mississippi where he began selling his paintings at age 15. He draws from his working experience on farms and ranches as a young man, and excels in award-winning western-themed art that can be found in galleries world-wide. His work is also featured on greeting cards (Leanin' Tree), commemorative plates (Franklin Mint), book covers, and even playing cards and T-shirts. Educated in Mississippi, Adams holds a Bachelor of Fine Arts in Advertising Design from the University of Southern Mississippi.

Since 1984 this fine artist has enjoyed living in the Prescott area where he has a studio at 506 Westwood Drive. He can be reached at 520/776-8211, or visit his website: www.hermonadams.com.

CLOUD DANCER

PAINTING: Hermon Adams

LOCATION: Prescott Resort

SNOW WOLF

ARTIST:　　Hermon Adams

LOCATION: Prescott Resort

THE CHALLENGE

ARTIST: Hermon Adams

LOCATION: Prescott Resort

THE PAINTING

Dedicated in 1969, this painting is a vibrant oil on canvas of the Smoki People at their pueblo, performing a ceremonial snake dance. It was presented to the City of Prescott by the Smoki (pronounced "smoke-eye") people, a group of local businessmen and women who were active from the 1920s through the early 1990s. They performed a snake dance similar to that of the Hopi along with other ceremonial dances that included chanting, dance steps and drum rhythms. The Smoki people eventually shifted their emphasis to the Smoki Museum (see *Museums* section) where they put their personal collections on display and aided in developing the museum as a nonprofit organization.

THE ARTIST

Creston Baumgartner, who died in 1984, was a superb artist who painted life as he saw it in his own style of oil on canvas and water color. Originally from Maryland, he graduated from the Maryland Institute of Fine Arts in Baltimore in 1927, then did post-graduate study at the Academy of Fine Arts in Philadelphia. In 1932 *Nature Magazine* sent him to Phoenix to research cover art, and he decided to stay. Creston and a friend founded the first art school there while he did freelance work. In 1947 the artist and his family moved to Prescott where he taught art and became active in the community. For almost 30 years he raised his family in the mile-high city, all the while painting and teaching his skills to both adults and children. As a long-time member of the Smoki People, he was asked to create the mural we see today in City Hall. Its colors have lost none of their vividness, and the figures are as impressive as they day they were painted. Most of the artist's work is in private collections, but the city of Prescott is fortunate to have this fine mural on display.

SMOKI PEOPLE OF PRESCOTT

ARTIST: Creston Baumgartner

LOCATION: Prescott City Hall

THE PAINTINGS

Buffalo Dancer is a 7'2" x 3'8" oil on canvas painted in 1919. This marvelous painting is detailed, expressive, and lit with color. *Kopi Butterfly, Migration* and *Return of the Kachinas,* all located in the Smoki Museum, are large and impressive expressions of artist Cory's love of the Native American people. In addition to the paintings shown in this book, a small oil by Cory entitled *Wu-Wu Ceremony* can be seen on the back wall of the Smoki Museum just above the door.

Two paintings, *Carding Wool* and *Indian Gathering,* located in the Prescott Public Library's Southwest Room, are not as grand in scale as the large pieces mentioned above, but are nevertheless impressive. *Migration of the Hopi Tribe in the Early 20th Century,* located in the First Congregational Church at 216 East Gurley Street, is a large piece done is soft colors that was dedicated in 1939. If you wish to see this painting, which is located in an upstairs hall, please first call the church at 445-4555.

THE ARTIST

Kate J. Cory lived and painted in Prescott from 1912-1958. Her talent, travel throughout the Southwest and great love of the Hopi people resulted in many extraordinary paintings, several of which are available for public viewing in Prescott. Her art continues to be the focus of gallery and museum exhibits that feature early women artists of Arizona.

Additional information on Kate Cory can be found in the *Histories and Biographies* and *Museums* sections of this book.

BUFFALO DANCER

ARTIST: Kate J. Cory

LOCATION: Smoki Museum

CARDING WOOL

ARTIST: Kate J. Cory

LOCATION: Prescott Public Library Southwest Room

INDIAN GATHERING

ARTIST: Kate J. Cory

LOCATION: Prescott Public Library Southwest Room

KOPI BUTTERFLY

ARTIST: Kate J. Cory

LOCATION: Smoki Museum

MIGRATION

ARTIST: Kate J. Cory

LOCATION: Smoki Museum

MIGRATION OF THE HOPI TRIBE IN THE EARLY 20ᵗʰ CENTURY

ARTIST: Kate J. Cory

LOCATION: First Congregational Church
216 East Gurley Street
Call 445-4555 to see painting.

RETURN OF THE KACHINAS

ARTIST: Kate J. Cory

LOCATION: Smoki Museum

THE PAINTINGS

William Hickling Prescott by Paul Coze in the Prescott City Hall council chambers is a beautiful portrait of the man after whom the city of Prescott was named and is unusual in that it is set in an ornate wooden frame painted by Coze. At the bottom is a plaque that reads, *William Hickling Prescott, 1796-1859. Brilliant american historian whose works inspired the naming of this city.* The council chambers is also home to a large Coze mural painted in 1963 that graces the far wall as one enters the room. It depicts life in the rich land and traditions of Prescott: towering pines; a cattle drive; schools, artists and musicians; lakes and granite boulders; summer camps; and Gambel quail, deer, and the mischievous roadrunner. Another piece--a grand eight-panel mural entitled *Prelude to Modern Prescott*--can be found in the conference room of the Phippen Museum. This extraordinary oil and acrylic painting combines scenes of trappers, mountain men, prospectors, soldiers, and residents of Prescott as the area developed from 1840 to 1900. It is framed with local gravel, sand, stones and mosaic pieces.

THE ARTIST

Paul Coze was a western artist, writer and sculptor who created exceptional pieces of art that can be seen not only in Prescott but throughout Phoenix and in different parts of the state. A partial listing of his work and further information about the artist can be found in the *Histories and Biographies* section under the heading *Paul Coze.*

LARGE MURAL ON CANVAS

ARTIST: Paul Coze

LOCATION: Prescott City Hall Council Chambers

Detail from City Hall mural.

PRELUDE TO MODERN PRESCOTT

ARTIST: Paul Coze

LOCATION: Phippen Museum

Detail from mural.

WILLIAM HICKLING PRESCOTT

ARTIST: Paul Coze

LOCATION: Prescott City Hall Council Chambers

THE PAINTING

Tom Mix in a tuxedo isn't something you see too often. This fine acrylic and oil rendering is artist Cheryl Foley's interpretation of the gentleman western movie star and performer who lived on the Bar-Circle-A ranch in Prescott, which is now home to the Ramada Resort and Spa and the Yavapai Hills residential area. While you're in the Ramada, look at the nice collection of western paintings in the Lariat Dining Room. Also notice the stained glass above the doors; there is more stained glass in the lobby.

THE ARTIST

Cheryl Foley is a local artist originally from Pennsylvania, where, in 1970, she graduated from the Moore College of Art in Philadelphia. She currently holds a B.F.A. in Illustration. Cheryl has worked in movie advertising, graphic arts and, as Foley Design, produced hand-painted clothing that was sold exclusively by Nordstrom. She has produced numerous murals, decorative wall painting, and fine art for businesses and private homes. Currently working as an interior design artist in the Prescott area, she can be reached at 520/778-5936.

TOM MIX

ARTIST: Cheryl Foley

LOCATON: Ramada Resort and Spa

THE PAINTINGS

On the walls of the Hassayampa Inn's Arizona Room are two large acrylic murals painted on plaster that can be seen when the room is not being used for a private party. These colorful murals, painted in 1978 by artist Ronald Hedge, depict several of northern Arizona's most visited natural wonders, including the Grand Canyon, Monument Valley, Sedona's red rock vistas, Sunset Crater, and of course Prescott's Thumb Butte. In addition, the Arizona Room, which served as a chapel is the 1970s, is home to several lovely stained-glass windows. In the lobby is another wall painting above the fireplace by artist Hedge. The lobby also boasts of a lovely hand-painted ceiling and an antique piano.

THE ARTIST

Ronald Hedge could not be located.

Detail from Arizona Room murals.

HASSAYAMPA MURALS

PAINTER: Ronald Hedge

LOCATION: Hassayampa Inn
              122 East Gurley

Lobby painting.

THE PAINTING

This approximately 15-foot-square wall painting is done in acrylic and depicts characters from the 1972 movie *Junior Bonner* starring Steve McQueen. It is a composite of photos found in the basement of The Palace Restaurant and Saloon just before the painting was started in 1990.

THE ARTIST

Vincent Hovley, whose signature reads "Hooley," is world-traveled artist who resides in Prescott but has his studio in California. His work, which he describes as the "rogue approach to art" changes with each subject. His work in oils has appeared in *Arizona Highways* magazine and can be found from France to Mexico. He recently completed a painting of the 1900 Prescott fire. For more information on artist Hovley, log on to www.bigshotartists.com.

JUNIOR BONNER MURAL

PAINTER: Vincent Michael Hovley

LOCATION: The Palace Restaurant and Saloon
120 South Montezuma Street

THE PAINTING

Prescott 1900 is a beautifully executed painting of early downtown Prescott that covers an entire wall in the Wells Fargo Bank Building in Frontier Village. Originally painted for the Wells Fargo building on Cortez Street in downtown Prescott, it was painstakingly removed and refurbished before being relocated to its present site. As you gaze at this colorful portrayal of Montezuma Street and Courthouse Plaza as it appeared at the turn of the century, try to imagine yourself walking right into the painting and joining the figures strolling down the street. If you have a keen eye, try to locate the well-hidden poodle that was intentionally painted into the scene.

THE ARTIST

Charles E. Kemp is no longer alive to charm us with his wit and talent.

PRESCOTT 1900

ARTIST: Charles E. Kemp

LOCATION: Wells Fargo Bank Building
              Frontier Village Shopping Center

Detail from *Prescott 1900*.

THE PAINTINGS

Grand Canyon was first displayed in the Prescott Resort in 1990. This fine oil is a 60" x 72" canvas executed in the old masters smooth brush technique. It depicts a panorama of the Grand Canyon as viewed from the Abyss Overlook on the South Rim.

Mustangs, the second Fred Lucas painting to be seen in the Resort, is a marvelous action-filled scene of stallions and mares running wild and free across the western plains as they have for hundreds of years.

THE ARTIST

Fred Lucas, an accomplished western artist, has his home and studio in the hills near Prescott, Arizona. Born in Tacoma, Washington, Lucas began his art education at the young age of nine. He studied at the Famous Artist Schools of Westport, Connecticut, and launched his career as a full-time fine arts painter in 1972 with gallery exhibits in Santa Fe, New Mexico, and Scottsdale, Arizona. Today he is considered to be one of the finest painters of the Grand Canyon and the American West. His portrayal of wild life, portraits and historical events have won him acclaim world-wide, and his work can be found in the Arizona State Capitol building and numerous museums, galleries and major hotels. When the elder George Bush was President of the United States, Lucas' work was seen on the walls of the White House. Much of Lucas' work is private collections. He can be reached at (520)632-7879.

GRAND CANYON

ARTIST: Fred Lucas

LOCATION: Prescott Resort

(Fred Lucas)

MUSTANGS

ARTIST: Fred Lucas

LOCATION: Prescott Resort

(Fred Lucas)

Out where the handclasp's a little
  stronger,
Out where the smile dwells a little
  longer,
That's where the West begins.
(Arthur Chapman, *Out Where the
  West Begins*)

THE PAINTINGS

A Little Girl From Cameron, Prescott Princess and *On Top of the World* are but three of George Molnar's incredibly life-like oil paintings that have become his trademark. As one gazes at these beautiful young Native American women, the light seems to come from everywhere—and nowhere. It takes a while to realize that the light comes from the artist's brushes. Mr. Molnar captures the beauty of every detail within the paintings—from wisps of hair to folds in the clothing and rocks. These are images that will stay with the viewer for a very long time.

THE ARTIST

George Molnar lives in the Prescott area where he continues to paint his beloved Navajo people. Raised in California, he began drawing at an early age and was delighted to be accepted into the Minneapolis-based Art Instruction Schools when he was just a high school freshman. While attending college he became interested in the Southwest landscape and the Native American people. After moving to Arizona he began visiting the vast Navajo reservation in the Four Corners region where he established a trust with the people he met, eventually sketching and photographing them for his paintings.

George Molnar portrays the Navajo with sensitivity and caring. His colorful, realistic paintings have gained world-wide recognition. For more information on the artist and his work log on to www.georgemolnar.com and www.ilovethewest.com.

A LITTLE GIRL FROM CAMERON

ARTIST: George Molnar

LOCATION: Prescott Resort

(George Molnar)

ON TOP OF THE WORLD

ARTIST: George Molnar

LOCATION: Prescott Resort

PRESCOTT PRINCESS

PAINTER: George Molnar

LOCATION: Prescott Resort

(George Molnar)

THE PAINTING

The Walker Party is a beautiful oil rendering that commemorates the arrival of some of the first men to what is today the City of Prescott. This painting, which is hung just around the corner from the Prescott Public Library's book store, must be studied closely for its fine detail and many figures. It was presented to the library in 1965 when it was part of a large exhibit of Phippen's work that was on display in the upstairs meeting room.

THE ARTIST

George Phippen was one of the area's best-known and loved western artists for many years before his death in 1965. He was one of the founders of the Cowboy Artists of America, and lived with his family in Skull Valley. For more information on this artist, see the *Histories and Biographies* and *Museums* sections of this book.

THE WALKER PARTY

ARTIST: George Phippen

LOCATION: Prescott Public Library

In creating, the only hard thing's to
  begin;
A grass-blade's no easier to make
  than an oak;
If you've once found the way, you've
  achieved the grand stroke.
(J. R. Lowell, *A Fable for Critics*, 1 534)

3. Other Treasures

Pieces of art not mentioned elsewhere in this book but worth a visit can be found at the following locations:

Embry-Riddle Aeronautical University

In addition to the two sculptures mentioned on pages 18 and 51, several smaller pieces can be seen on the walkway between Buildings 17 and 19 where *Eagle* by John Dobberteen is located. In addition, there is a bronze memorial, *Icarus*, located next to the parking lot in front of the bookstore.

Forest Villas Hotel

In the elegant lobby of the Forest Villas Hotel is a beautiful 16th Century tapestry. Also to be seen and appreciated in the hotel is a Louis XVI desk.

Granite Creek Mural

Students from Prescott's Mile High Middle School have painted a mural along Granite Creek on the retaining wall below the Bank of America building thatt chronicles the changes of the Granite Creek area throughout the history of Prescott. In preparing to paint the mural the students thoroughly researched the Granite Creek area, visiting the Sharlot Hall Museum, talking to members of the Yavapai-Prescott Native American Tribe, and interviewing people who have lived along the creek for 25 years or more. Local artist Elizabeth Newman of the Living Folklore Society worked with the Prescott Creeks Preservation Association in designing the mural and preparing the students to paint this colorful new addition to the Prescott art scene.

Heritage Park Zoo

A giant preying mantis fashioned out of steel has been installed on the zoo grounds. This piece, made of linear steel formed into 24 modules and bolted together, is 43 feet long, 27 feet tall, and weighs 2,800 pounds. The sculptor, Ruben Bogunia of Prescott, constructed this very large insect at Ohio University in 1975, and it was located at a private residence in Cleveland for 22 years before being moved to Prescott. Bogunia disassembled the mantis in 2000, put the sections on a flat-bed truck, and brought them to Prescott. Here he overhauled the piece and modified it to meet current code. The mantis legs are 10 feet long, and they extend four feet underground. The sculpture is wearing two new coats of oil-based primer and one of a reddish-orange latex that will help the surface withstand the temperature extremes of high mountain life. Bogunia, who also did the new front entrance gate of the zoo, can be reached at his place of business entitled "Maximum Torch, Will Travel," (520)636-0776.

Hotel St. Michael

In addition to the St. Michael's interesting and historic interior, there's an unusual painting high on the wall of the café: an excellent reproduction of Rembrandt's *The Sampling Officials of the Draper's Guild*. The original, which hangs in the Rijksmuseum in Amsterdam, The Netherlands, was painted in 1662 by Rembrandt van Rijn. The origin of this painting in the hotel is not known. Other paintings can be found throughout the hotel.

Prescott College

Prescott College has three large murals painted on building walls that are visible to the public. One is on the side of the Butte Creek Café, 217 Garden Street; the second on the Summit Arts Building at 112 Summit Avenue; and the third is on the Sinagua Building at 322 Grove Street. These murals, painted by students, are colorful and eye-catching.

Prescott Public Library

On an outside wall that faces the library's lower level parking area is a colorful mural by artist Tony Cocilovo that was painted in 1993 as a result of his winning a competition. It depicts an Arizona landscape as viewed from an ancient Native American Indian pueblo. Three old pots taken from actual photos are also featured. Cocilovo, a Prescott resident, also painted the striking portrait of Sharlot Hall that can be seen in the Sharlot Hall Museum's Administration and Exhibit Building (see page 204). A fine oil rendering of Sheriff Buckey O'Neill, based on an actual photograph, is featured on page 208. Cocilovo can be reached at (520)445-1643.

(Tony Cocilovo)

Prescott Resort

The resort has an excellent display of art in its corridors at all times of the year. In addition to the paintings on permanent display by Hermon Adams, Fred Lucas and George Molnar, be sure to notice *Big Country Small Talk* by Bill Anton and *R.O. Ranch* by Ray Swanson. If you walk into the lounge and look high above the fireplace, you will see *Eagle's Nest*, a 7.5 x 2.5-foot welded steel eagle created by local artist and musician W. C. (Willy) Rubottom. Rubottom has also created an 8½-foot female and 9½-foot male miner out of welded pure copper rod that can be found in the city of Bagdad, Arizona. He can be reached at (520)445-8047.

(Pamela DeMarais)

Oft in the stilly night,
  Ere slumber's chain has bound me,
Fond memory brings the light
  Of other days around me;
    The smiles, the tears,
    of boyhood's years,
The words of love then spoken;
    The eyes that shone
    Now dimmed and gone,
The cheerful hearts now broken.
(Thomas Moore, *Oft in the Stilly Night*)

4. Museums

Prescott boasts of three excellent museums, with a fourth being planned for the year 2001. The largest of the current museums is the **Sharlot Hall Museum**, located in the downtown area on Gurley Street, and named after its founder, Sharlot M. Hall. The **Phippen Museum**, sitting atop a picturesque hill seven miles north of Courthouse Plaza on Highway 89, is named after western artist George Phippen. The **Smoki Museum-American Art and Culture**, located just east of downtown Prescott's town center off Gurley Street, was established by and named after the Smoki People. The newest addition to the roster, to be called the **Fort Whipple Interpretive Center**, due to be open in 2001, will be housed in Building 11 of the Northern Arizona VA Healthcare System just north of the Highway 69-89 junction off Highway 89.

There is much to be learned from the exhibits and collections in each of these fine museums. Adults and children who want to know more about Prescott, Yavapai County, the State of Arizona, and the amazing and diverse Southwest should visit the facilities listed below.

> **Sharlot Hall Museum**
> **Phippen Museum**
> **Smoki Museum-American Art and Culture**
> **Fort Whipple Interpretive Center**

Territorial Governor's Mansion.
(Pamela DeMarais)

John C. Frémont House.
(Pamela DeMarais)

SHARLOT HALL MUSEUM
415 West Gurley Street
Prescott, AZ 86301
(520)445-3122
www.sharlot.org

Open: 10:00 am - 5:00 pm, Monday-Saturday (Apr-Oct)
10:00 am - 4:00 pm, Monday-Saturday (Nov-Mar)
1:00 pm - 5:00 pm, Sunday
Closed: Thanksgiving, Christmas, New Year's Day

Admission: Donation requested

Situated on three acres of land only two blocks from Courthouse Square, the **Sharlot Hall Museum** is one of the most beautiful and historically important museums in all of the Southwest. Founded in 1928 and championed by pioneer historian Sharlot M. Hall, this museum consists of nine buildings plus a gift shop, outdoor amphitheater, and outdoor display of antique mining machinery. On the landscaped grounds are the Pioneer Vegetable Garden, Ethnobotanical Herb Garden, and Memorial Rose Garden. Trees and shrubs are identified with small placards. Primary buildings located on the grounds are the following:

Administration and Exhibit Building
William C. Bashford House (1877) (gift shop)
Fort Misery (1863)
John C. Frémont House (1875)
Ranch House (replica)
School House (replica)
Sharlot Hall Building (1934)
Territorial Governor's Mansion (1864)
Transportation building (1910)

This fine museum also houses a large archives that is open to the public. Within the archives can be found a 10,000-volume library, thousands of historic photos, an extensive subject index, manuscripts, genealogical resources, oral history interviews, historical periodicals and area newspapers, old city and telephone directories, maps dating back to 1895, homestead records, cemetery information, and district surveys.

Major events held at the **Sharlot Hall Museum** include the Folk Music Festival, Folk Arts Fair, Prescott Indian Art Market, and Arizona Cowboy Poets Gathering. Major exhibits change periodically in the main Exhibit Building and the Sharlot Hall Building. During the Christmas season both the Governor's Mansion and the Frémont House are decorated in the tradition of the late 1800s. Other buildings sporting holiday decor are the Sharlot Hall Building, the Museum Center foyer, and the Bashford House solarium. On one evening early in December costumed folk representing the first residents of the area sing carols and talk to visitors about Christmases of yore.

Just a few of the other activities sponsored by Sharlot Hall Museum are the following:

- Field trips to places of historic significance
- Regularly scheduled lectures
- Living history programs featuring staff and volunteers
- History under the stars - summer outdoor theater presenting stories from area history

Expansion plans are underway for the first decade of the 21st Century for new and larger facilities.

William C. Bashford House.
(Pamela DeMarais)

Fort Misery.
(Pamela DeMarais)

Phippen Museum.

View from Phippen Museum.

PHIPPEN MUSEUM
4701 North Highway 89
Prescott, AZ 86301
(520)778-1385   fax (520)778-4524
www.phippenmuseum.org

Open: 10:00 am - 4:00 pm daily; 1:00 pm - 4:00 pm Sunday. Closed Tuesdays all year. Also closed Thanksgiving, Christmas, and New Year's.

Admission: yes

In 1974 a group of local art enthusiasts dreamed of establishing a western art museum in Prescott. Louise Phippen agreed to let them use the name of her late artist husband, George Phippen, in establishing such a museum, and thus the Phippen Museum opened in 1984. Its focus is on traditional art of the American West, and within its walls are art and artifacts relating to George Phippen, including three of his beautiful bronzes: *Father (Padre) Eusebio Francisco Kino, Arizona Rock Hopper,* and *Father Kino and Boy.* (See *Histories and Biographies* section under the heading *George Phippen.*)

In the museum's Community Cultural Center is an amazing eight-panel mural entitled *Prelude to Modern Prescott* painted by artist Paul Coze (see *Histories and Biographies* section under the heading *Paul Coze*). The mural, painted in 1963, was commissioned by the City of Prescott to commemorate its 100th anniversary. It includes individual panels entitled: *Trappers, explorers, mountain men, Ca 1840; Gold, magnet of men, 1863; Fort Whipple, a frontier post in the land of the Yavapai, summer 1864; Prescott—Arizona's First Capital, fall 1864; First rodeo, July 4th, 1888; Whiskey Row, winter 1896; Home of the brave, August 1898; and Garden party, spring 1900.* Each panel was framed by Coze in local stones, gravel and sand, with some mosaic tile.

Among other works of art in the Phippen Museum's permanent collection are a bronze recast of Frederic Remington's *Coming Through the Rye,* and a bronze entitled *The Only Good Indian Is...* by

Maher Naguib Morcos. In addition to these pieces, a number of oil paintings depicting scenes of the west, including the large and impressive *Mongollon Rim* by artist David Caton and *Solitude* by Olaf Wieghorst, are held in the permanent collection.

In front of the museum are a covered wagon and buckboard that date back to the mid-1900s, large metal animal sculptures, and antique farm and ranch equipment. The museum's location offers the visitor a panoramic view of Prescott's dramatic Granite Dells.

The Phippen Museum has an excellent museum store that features the work of more than 100 Arizona artists, and each year over Memorial Day weekend the museum presents its famous outdoor show and sale in Prescott's Courthouse Plaza. This is a juried show that is recognized as one of the top ten outdoor art shows in the country. For three days over 150 of the nation's finest artists exhibit and sell their fine art of the American West. There is no admission.

Padre Kino bronze by George Phippen.

Two panels from *Prelude to Modern Prescott*
by Paul Coze.

Smoki Museum.

SMOKI MUSEUM
AMERICAN ART AND CULTURE
147 North Arizona Street
Prescott, AZ 86304
520/445-1230
smoki@futureone.com   www.smoki.com

Open: 10:00 am - 4:00 pm, Mon.-Sat. (Apr. 15 - Oct. 31)
10:00 am - 4:00 pm, Sat. and 1:00 pm - 4:00 pm Sun.
(Nov. 1 - Apr. 14)
Closed Easter, Christmas Eve and Day, New Year's Day

Admission: yes

Visitors to the **Smoki Museum-American Art & Culture** will be rewarded with a rich display of baskets, pottery dating from pre-Columbian to present day, kachinas, textiles, beadwork, headdresses, and more. Paintings by Kate Cory, an artist who lived with the Hopi Indians in the early 1900s, are also a part of this large collection (see *Histories and Biographies section* under heading *Kate Cory*). The interior of the museum is fashioned after a Hopi Pueblo and contains a Zuni-style fireplace.

This nonprofit museum was started by the Smoki (pronounced "smoke-eye") People, a group of local businessmen who began performing their version of the snake dance and other ceremonial of Southwestern Indian tribes. The Smoki people were active from 1921 until the early 1990s. They stopped their performances in 1990. The museum was opened to the public in 1935 and housed in the unique native granite stone structure that you see today. Personal collections belonging to members, along with artifacts excavated from Prescott-area archaeological sites, are permanently displayed in this unusual museum, as well as new and changing exhibits.

The **Smoki Museum** has an extensive research library, and a gift shop that offers a wide variety of handcrafted Indian jewelry, pottery, baskets and other items, as well as a comprehensive selection of books on Native American topics. It also offers a popular series of Sunday afternoon lectures, and features Native American artists-in-residence during the year—including a Native American rug auction. Guided tours for schoolchildren and other groups are available year-round by appointment, and a school outreach program is offered to area schools. The museum is also active in supporting local archaeological digs.

3,000-year-old bent twig figure.

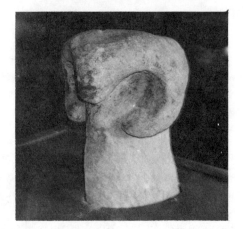

One of two stone rams heads found in the earth at Prescott Fairgrounds site in 1935. Age estimated at 800-1000 years.

Apache baskets, late 1800s.

Yavapai baskets, early 1900s.

Building 11 that will house the
Fort Whipple Interpretive Center.

FORT WHIPPLE
INTERPRETIVE CENTER
Northern Arizona VA Healthcare System
500 Highway 89 North
Prescott, AZ 86313

Museum will be open the summer of 2001.

When the Interpretive Center opens in the former officers' quarters, it will be the culmination of a cooperative effort by the Sharlot Hall Museum and the Northern Arizona VA Healthcare System. Initial museum exhibits will feature topical looks at the history connected with the facility from its inception as a frontier military post in 1864 to its current service to America's veterans. Future exhibitions will expand this interpretation as the rich history, both military and medical, is presented through text, photographs and artifacts related to Fort Whipple and the Hospital. In addition, the Fort Whipple Frontier Regulars, dressed in accurate reproductions of period clothing and accessories (jewelry, armaments, etc.), will oftentimes be on the grounds to greet and talk to visitors (see page 118).

Now known simply as "Building 11," the structure is being restored to its 1912-1920 appearance. Yellow with green trim (original colors) and a big front porch, Building 11 can be found in the area of the officers' quarters on the south side of the Veterans Center.

One can gain access to the scenic grounds of the Veterans Center by driving east from Prescott's downtown area, and following the signs for Highway 89 North. About ½ mile north of the 89-69 junction is a left-hand turn that leads into the grounds. Please drive slowly and with respect through this picturesque and historic site. Also be aware that this is an active medical center, and that elderly patients are often crossing the streets. Patients in wheelchairs also navigate the grounds. Speed limits are strictly enforced. Fort Whipple is a designated Historic District on the National Register of Historic Places. Further information on Fort Whipple can be found in the *Histories and Biographies* section.

Fort Whipple Frontier Regulars on the steps of Building 11
of the Fort Whipple Interpretive Center. L-R: Yisrael Yitzhak
Ben-David, Scott Seyler, Ron Anderson and Barbara Anderson.
(Barbara Anderson)

5. Histories and Biographies

Significant areas of local interest and several renowned men and women who contributed to the art and history of Prescott and northern Arizona deserve an expanded description. The following histories and biographies can be found in this section:

HISTORIES

Fine Art Metal Casting
Fort Whipple
Prescott, Arizona
   Historic Buildings
   Victorian Homes
   Cemeteries
Yavapai-Prescott Native American Indians

BIOGRAPHIES

Solon Hannibal Borglum
Mary Elizabeth Jane Colter
Kate Cory
Paul Coze
Sharlot Mabridth Hall
William Owen "Buckey" O'Neill
George Phippen

A. ***Making the rubber mold.*** Diane Simpson of Thumb
Butte Bronze applying silicone rubber to a life-size foal
original clay. Sculpture by Diane Simpson. (Diane Simpson)

B. ***Pouring the wax:*** Jeff Caron pouring liquid wax into
a silicone rubber mold at Artscape Bronze Casting.

FINE ART METAL CASTING

Residents of Prescott and visitors alike pause daily in Courthouse Plaza to gaze upon three fine monumental bronzes: *All Veterans Memorial, Cowboy at Rest,* and the *William O'Neill Rough Rider Monument.* A short distance from Courthouse Plaza stand the impressive *Early Rodeo* and *Early Settlers.* These and numerous other cast metal pieces in and around Prescott are featured in the *Sculptures* section of this book.

These beautiful works are amazing to behold. The men and women who designed and followed their pieces through to the final finishing are true masters of their craft. Bronzes come in all sizes, from larger-than-life monumental works to small medals. All have been cast in a foundry. Many of the pieces featured in this book were cast locally, others as far away as New York. The process is long and complicated, and few people are aware of the work involved in casting a piece such as *Leaps and Bounds,* the animated bronze frog that graces the Yavapai College Sculpture Garden, or *Silver Tornado,* the large stainless steel bull that resides in front of the Yavapai Regional Medical Center. This section will briefly attempt to explain the process of bronze casting.

The Prescott area is home to five foundries: Skurja Art Castings and Thumb Butte Bronze in Prescott; Bronzesmith and Dykeman in Prescott Valley; and Century Reproductions in Dewey. Nearby Sedona is home to Artscape Bronze Casting. All are actively involved in daily preparation of ceramic and/or rubber molds, pouring and finishing waxes, pouring molten bronze or other metals, finishing, applying patinas, numbering editions, and delivering the finished product. Before the foundry can begin its work, however, artists must sculpt the original piece from clay, plaster, wood, wax or stone. Artists work closely with foundry personnel to ensure that their pieces turn out to be exactly as they had envisioned them, or even better due to the experience of metal experts.

Bronze casting is an ancient art. Bronze itself is an alloy made from copper, tin, zinc, and other trace metals. Copper alone is too soft for practical use; the addition of tin and zinc make it hard enough to be made into bells, bearings, wire, armaments and decorative objects, among others. Coins have always been stamped. The earliest use of bronze was in the Middle East, dating from about 5000 BC (BCE), when copper was mixed with arsenic. For almost 3,000 years, beginning in 4000 BC (BCE) during what was called the Bronze Age, copper and bronze were the main metals used for making tools, weapons, bowls, pots, and other implements. When iron was introduced around 1000 BC (BCE), the Bronze Age ended and the Iron Age began.

Bronze and other metals have to be cast (poured) in a molten state. Coin blanks, for example, are made from molds that are filled with molten metal. The two basic art bronzes used today are called *Everdur* and *Herculoy*. *Everdur* bronze is 95% copper, 4.08% silicon, .03% tin, .01% zinc, .01% lead, .02% iron, .02% nickel, .007% aluminum, and 1.04% manganese. *Herculoy* bronze is 92% copper, 4% silicon, and 4% zinc. Copper mixed only with zinc results in brass.

Museums around the world are full of beautiful old bronzes that were cast in Italy, Egypt and Greece. Syria, Nigeria, China, India— all have produced exotic figures that date back thousands of years. Large figures, small pieces, and even giant doors found in Italian cathedrals have been cast from the magic ingredients: copper plus zinc, tin, and other metals. Leonardo Da Vinci worked in bronze; so did Rodin and Michaelangelo. Today's foundries carry on the tradition of the masters with their fine and detailed work.

One method of casting, called the *lost wax* method, is a straightforward gravity-pour process that has been used for thousands of years. Briefly, the steps involved in casting wax with **slosh rubber molds** are as follows:

- The original sculpture is covered with silicone rubber (4-6 coats) (on one half and then the other) that sets to create a mold (A). A layer of plaster is applied over the silicone to stiffen the exterior.

- The rubber is removed in two pieces, bound together, and filled with melted wax that is sloshed around and then poured out. This is done several times to create a hollow wax (B).

- After the wax hardens, the mold is removed and the wax image carefully touched up to remove seam lines or imperfections (C). Other wax parts such as arms or legs are attached.

- The wax is then gated (sprued/vented) to create channels for the molten bronze to reach every part of the mold and to carry out escaping gases and air when the bronze is being poured (D).

- The gated wax is first dipped in a citrus and alcohol wash to remove grease, oils and dirt, then dipped into a slurry. To create the ceramic shell mold, the wax is dipped repeatedly first in slurry then in silica sand, with the piece being allowed to dry between dippings (E).

- After the ceramic shell dries and hardens, it is turned upside-down, heated, and the wax burned out in a 1600°F furnace. The wax is retrieved for future use.

- The molten bronze, heated from 1750°F to 2050°F, is cast (poured) into the preheated shell mold (F).

- After the bronze has cooled, the ceramic shell is broken off in many pieces (G).

What emerges is the bronze casting, which is ready for finishing. This includes sandblasting away any remaining bits of ceramic shell and smoothing out irregularities. Gates are removed with a carbon arc torch or other cutting methods. With larger pieces, separate parts or sections are joined by welding. After the bronze has all parts joined and all imperfections removed, the metal is heated with a blowtorch to 200-300°F and the patina (color) applied using chemicals that are brushed, sprayed or airbrushed on (H). The final step in completing the bronze is waxing or applying lacquer to seal it.

A second type of mold, called an *injection rubber mold,* is different from the slosh mold in that it is generally smaller and is injected with liquid wax under pressure instead of being poured. This results is a finely detailed product such as bird feathers or other objects that have delicate and fragile patterns. This type of mold produces jewelry-quality castings done on a foundry scale (I).

The piece to be cast is suspended in a box structure that is then filled with a platinum cure silicone rubber. After the rubber has set, the box is removed and the rubber cut away in two pieces, using a scallop motion. These two pieces are then interlocked and bound together, and the liquid wax injected (J). After it has hardened, the wax pattern is removed and mounted vertically in a perforated stainless steel cylinder. High-refractory plaster is then pumped in under vacuum (to eliminate air bubbles). After the plaster has set, the cylinder is placed in a kiln where the wax is melted out at low temperature (typically 48 hours) while the plaster is curing. Once cured, the plaster mold is turned upright and placed in a vacuum chamber where the bronze or silver is poured. The resulting piece is oftentimes a finely detailed part of a larger bronze that will be attached by welding or soldering.

A third method of casting, typically used when softer metals like pewter, pewter/bronze alloy, or zinc are being cast, is simply to pour these low temperature molten alloys directly into a specially formulated silicone mold. The mold will usually hold up for 20-25 castings. Original artists' sculptures are used to make the molds, as in the hot wax method of casting, but because the molten metal is poured directly into a reusable mold, the end product is less expensive. Milled (crushed) porcelain mixed with casting material is another medium poured in this manner. This process is often used for miniatures that are sold in limited editions by businesses such as movie studios, wildlife conservation groups and museums, although larger pieces—even life-size—can also be cast. Each piece is done by hand and the detail, especially on miniatures, is very fine (K). Many artists have their work cast both in hot bronze and then in a softer alloy for limited edition distribution.

Skurja Art Castings in Prescott, Bronzesmith in Prescott Valley, and Artscape Bronze Casting in Sedona offer tours by appointment only. Bronzesmith also features a large gallery of its artists' work.

Prescott Area

Bronzesmith Fine Art Foundry
and Gallery
7331 East 2nd Street
Prescott Valley, AZ 86314
(520)772-2378
bronzart@primenet.com
www.bronzesmith.com

Century Reproductions
12151 East Highway 69
Dewey AZ 86327
(520)772-7300
www.centuryreproductions.com

Dykeman Art Foundry
8101 East Pecos Drive
Prescott Valley AZ 86314
(520)772-7950

Skurja Art Castings
1056 Spire Drive
Prescott AZ 86305
(520)778-3651

Thumb Butte Bronze
1701 West Adams
Prescott AZ 86303
(520)778-5273

Sedona

Artscape Bronze Casting
2107 Yavapai Drive
Sedona AZ 86336
(520)204-2913

C. *Touching up a wax.* Diane Simpson of
Thumb Butte Bronze removing imperfections.

D. *Gating:* Sean Parker at Bronzesmith gating waxes.
(Pamela DeMarais)

E. *Slurry Mold:* Drying ceramic shell molds at Skurja Art Castings.
These molds are the result of gated wax having been dipped a
number of times in a slurry and silica sand.

F. *Casting:* Pouring the molten bronze at Bronzesmith.
(Pamela DeMarais)

G. *Breaking out the shell:* Hammering off a ceramic
shell at Artscape Bronze Casting.

H. *Patina:* Scott McCormick of Skurja Art Castings heating the large bronze eagle *Out of the Blue* by artist Ken Rowe before applying the patina.

I. *Injection rubber mold.* L-R: original seashell, rubber mold with wax, and resulting bronze shell at Dykeman Art Foundry.

J. **Wax injection mold.** Marty Lopez of Dykeman Art Foundry injecting liquid wax into secured rubber mold.

K. Pewter and pewter/bronze pieces, including miniatures, cast by Century Reproductions.

Fort Whipple during the early years , c. 1900.
(Sharlot Hall Museum, Prescott, Arizona)

Fort Whipple (Department of Veterans Affairs Northern
Arizona Healthcare System) as it looks today.

FORT WHIPPLE

As late as 1861 the Arizona Territory was virtually lawless. In the southern part of the state around Tucson there was talk of secession and a lot of pro-Confederate sympathies. When the Civil War started the few Federal troops stationed in present-day Arizona were sent to defend Union forces in the Rio Grande Valley, and civilians were left to fend for themselves, especially against the Indians. In 1862 Union troops arrived from California, led by General James Carleton, who secured the area in and around Tucson. He declared Arizona to be subject to a military government, and Camp Lowell and Fort Bowie were established. Carleton then moved east to become military commander of New Mexico.

In 1863 General Carleton established Fort Whipple as a military post at a place called Del Rio Springs (today's Chino Valley). In 1864 its location was moved to the site of today's Prescott Veterans Affairs Center off Highway 89 just north of downtown Prescott. The fort was named after Brigadier General Amiel W. Whipple, who led an expedition into Arizona in 1853-54 and later died from wounds received at the Civil War battle of Chancellorsville, Virginia. The original fort construction was a wooden stockade consisting of several buildings.

When Governor John Goodwin and other government officials were making their way to the Arizona Territory in 1863, they met up with General Carleton in Santa Fe, New Mexico. It was General Carleton who advised Governor Goodwin to locate the seat of government at Prescott, near the recently established fort in Chino Valley. He recommended the area because its residents were not aligned with the Confederacy (although a few were suspect), and the land was rich in minerals and lumber.

Late in 1863 Major Edward B. Willis arrived in Chino Valley from Fort Union, New Mexico, with troops and supplies to set up camp and officially establish Fort Whipple as a military post. General

Carleton had requested and received two companies of infantry to be assigned to Fort Whipple to help control the problems of Indians attacking miners and homesteaders. Members of the Apache and Yavapai tribes periodically raided the countryside, killing miners and homesteaders and making off with the animals. They also raided supply wagons and attacked wagon trains.

Provisions were hard to come by in the early days of the fort, as the only regular transport into the area was by wagon train from New Mexico. Military campaigns against the Indians were often cut short or scuttled due to lack of supplies. The troops at Fort Whipple had great difficulty keeping up with the attacks as their numbers were small to begin with, and soldiers regularly left the Army when their enlistments were up to become miners. For example, in April 1864 there were 124 men on duty at Fort Whipple, but by October of that year there were only 24.

The soldiers who stayed at Fort Whipple led a spartan life. Food staples were limited and men often were sick as a result of their meager diets. Flapjacks fried in pork fat with coffee was a common meal. Milk, butter, eggs and chickens were rare commodities, and fresh vegetables were almost nonexistent. The most common ailments at Fort Whipple were fever, scurvy, and diarrhea.

In May of 1864 Major Willis moved his troops from Chino Valley to the new site of Fort Whipple just north of Prescott, where it remains today. After having built numerous structures in Chino Valley, he was not happy to have to start all over again. The fort needed to be located where the people and government were, however, so any objections were overcome.

The new Fort Whipple was the only stockade construction of 42 U.S. Army posts in Arizona. Of the 169 forts used by the U.S. Army west of the Mississippi from 1866-1886, only 18 had walls. Fort Whipple consisted of a 200-square-foot plaza surrounded by 12-foot-high pine logs that were buried 2 feet deep. The stockade contained officers' quarters, administrative offices, quartermaster and commissary supply store, an ammunition magazine, and soldiers' quarters. Entry was made through large heavy lumber gates. A flagpole and lone mountain howitzer stood in the center of the plaza. Also within the compound were a store and log houses for civilian employees. A hospital was built outside the stockade but within view of the sentinals. Also outside were corrals for animals and equipment buildings. Supplies were shipped in regularly by wagon from Yuma via Ehrenberg.

The military from Fort Whipple fought regularly with the Athabascan-speaking Apache warriors who sent out raiding parties in the area. The objective of the garrison was to protect people coming into the area from attack, and so skirmishes were regular and often. Negotiations were held from time to time between representatives of the U.S. Government and Apache chiefs, but little was accomplished. Neither side trusted the other, and meetings often ended in bloodshed. The Apaches resented Indian agents who treated them unfairly, and they didn't trust the Government's unreliable policies.

Among the many different tribes living in Arizona, the Pima and Maricopa were considered to be friendly to the Army since they were enemies of the Apache. Some Yavapai braves cooperated with the U.S. Army and were recruited as scouts and trackers. Many Army scouts were Apaches.

The year 1871 brought in one of the most famous military men of the time, General George Crook. Crook was a West Point man who was unique in that he saw the American Indian as a human being, not just as a red man or savage. He believed that force against the Indian was to be used only when necessary.

Crook had served in the Army for many years, having been in Company D, 4th Infantry in Oregon in 1857 where he was hit in the hip with an arrow in the Battle of Pit River Canyon. The head of the arrow could not be extracted. After serving in the Civil War from

1861-1864, he returned to the West, going first to Idaho and Nevada, then to Arizona.

When he arrived at Fort Whipple in 1871 there were ongoing negotiations between representatives of the U.S. Government and the Apaches, so General Crook held off taking any military action. By 1872, however, when peace negotiations had failed, Crook was ready to proceed.

After numerous battles, the last of the Yavapai surrendered in April 1873 and were interned on the Rio Verde and San Carlos reservations by Congressional order. The U.S. War Department turned over management of the reservations to the Department of Interior and their agents. Crook was no friend of the Indian agents, and accused them of mismanagement and plundering. He hoped the Yavapai people would live peaceably on the reservations and that the Government would keep its promises. In 1875 Crook left Fort Whipple after having been promoted to Brigadier General.

In 1870 when the Army had named Fort Whipple as the Headquarters for the Military Department of Arizona, many of the old buildings were torn down and replaced. Wooden buildings at the Fort, as in downtown Prescott, were prone to fire. In April 1872 several structures burned and were rebuilt. In October 1878 three sets of officers' quarters were destroyed by fire, and in 1881 the headquarters office building burned. During the years 1882-83 frame and adobe buildings replaced many of the older structures. Fort Whipple was just one of four Army posts in the area that were joined by what is still known as the General Crook trail. Other forts on the 200-mile-long trail that hugs the Mogollon Rim were Camp Verde in the Verde Valley (where many Indian captives were interned – see section on *The Yavapai-Prescott Native American Indians*), and Fort Apache in the White Mountains and Fort Defiance near Pinetop/Lakeside. U.S. Army troops and wagons used the trail for 22 years.

To aid in communications between Prescott and other important locations, a military telegraph line was put up that linked Fort Whipple, Camp Verde and Fort Apache with Phoenix, Tucson, Yuma and San Diego. The growing traffic between Army posts and Phoenix on the Black Canyon Highway created a need for public transportation. By 1878 a stagecoach made the run from Phoenix to Prescott.

One of the original entrance gates to Fort Whipple
(located in front of Yavapai College Performance Hall).

Life at Fort Whipple was hard work combined with numerous social events. The post commander led the way in establishing social gatherings, and if he were married, his wife had a say in what went on. General August V. Kautz, commander from 1874-1878, and his wife Fannie set a new standard with dances, theater, and numerous benefits. Both enlisted men and townfolk attended.

Life in Prescott and its immediate surroundings at this time in history was mostly enjoyable and often routine for the inhabitants. Away from town, however, and especially on the reservations, the situation was very difficult and often chaotic. Many of the problems were caused by the U.S. Government representatives—the Indian agents. Many of them were corrupt and had no real interest in the welfare of the people they were supposed to be helping.

In September 1882 General Crook was brought back to Fort Whipple to resolve recurring problems with the Indians. The Apaches on the Rio Verde reservation had been moved to the hot, dry San Carlos reservation, which caused resentment and great anger. Crook said that they had good reason to be upset, and that they had been victimized by the agents who regularly stole supplies meant for the Indians.

Many Apaches escaped from San Carlos and fled to the Sierra Madre Mountains of Mexico. They then came north across the border in periodic raiding parties. Crook went into Mexico, rounded up the wayward Apaches, and returned them to the reservation. Among them was the famous Geronimo.

In May 1885 Geronimo escaped and fled again to Mexico, and Crook ordered the Army to bring him back with the help of Apache scouts. Crook had an agreement with Geronimo that his life would be spared and that he would be held in prison for two years if he would surrender. Crook also promised not to kill the renegade braves if he came quietly. The following year Geronimo surrendered. While being returned to the reservation, however, he took advantage of a lapse in Army security and once more got away. President Cleveland ordered Crook to go after Geronimo and capture him once and for all, ignoring the previous agreement. Crook said no and asked to be relieved of his duty.

General Nelson Miles was then assigned to bring in Geronimo using only Government troops and no Indian scouts. After months of futile searching in Mexico, Miles brought in Apache scouts and located Geronimo who finally surrendered—this time for good. General Crook remained at Fort Whipple until the end of 1886.

At the end of the Apache wars the U.S. Government began to close some of the military posts. By September 1891 the following forts were abandoned: McDowell, Mojave, Lowell, Selden, Thomas, Verde and Union. Fort Whipple was discontinued (but not abandoned) in 1898 and regarrisoned in 1902. It was rebuilt in 1904 and finally abandoned in 1913. In 1922 it was given to the U.S. Public Health Service and made into a Veterans Administration Hospital for disabled veterans and men with tuberculosis. In 1959 it changed to a general medical and surgical center, and today it is officially named the Department of Veterans Affairs Northern Arizona Healthcare System.

One of Fort Whipple's more famous families was named LaGuardia. Fiorello LaGuardia, who was mayor of New York City in the 1930s, lived with his family in Prescott as a child from 1892-1898. He graduated from Prescott High School. His father was the 11th Infantry regimental bandmaster at Fort Whipple.

The *Museums* section of this book tells about the new Fort Whipple Interpretive Center that will be open to the public in late 2001.

Graduating class of Prescott High School, January 10, 1898.
Fiorello LaGuardia is third from the right in top row.
(Sharlot Hall Museum, Prescott, Arizona)

Whiskey Row in the late 1800s.
(Sharlot Hall Museum, Prescott, Arizona)

Whiskey Row as it appears today.

PRESCOTT, ARIZONA

The year was 1863 when a group of men led by mountain man Joe Reddeford Walker came to the Prescott area in search of gold. Walker had been prospecting in the San Francisco Mountains as early as 1861, but had been harassed by the Indians and left. He came to the Prescott area on the advice of General James Carleton, military commander of New Mexico, to set up a base camp in a potentially lucrative gold-producing area, and to seek military protection for mining claims.

Scout and trapper Pauline Weaver, who was already in Prescott in 1863 and had found gold, knew the territory well. He had been a member of the 1831 Ewing Young party that had trapped along the Salt and Verde Rivers and had included famed scout Kit Carson. When a major strike was made by the Walker party on Lynx Creek and by the Peeples party on Antelope Creek, word traveled fast—especially to the depleted gold fields of California. Gold was also found on Big Bug, Granite and Turkey creeks. The Pioneer Mining District was established, along with the Weaver Mining District, Yavapai Mining District, Walker Mining District, and Quartz Mining District. Gold-seekers began streaming into the area.

This was the time of the Civil War (1861-1865). The U.S. Congress and President Lincoln wanted to secure the Arizona Territory with its mineral riches for Union forces. The area now known as Prescott was chosen as Arizona's Territorial Capital and county seat because the only Arizona town with a significant population was Tucson, many residents of which had Confederate sympathies and dreams of secession. In 1863 General Carleton had established Camp Whipple at Del Rio Springs (now Chino Valley). It acted as the Territorial Government of Arizona from January 18 - May 18, 1864, then was relocated to a site just north of today's city of Prescott (see section on *Fort Whipple*). Carleton wanted the new territorial government to be located near the area's gold fields, not at the "insignificant village of Tucson." The census of 1864 gave Tucson a population of 1,586. The city of Phoenix did not yet exist.

The bill establishing Arizona as a territory passed the senate and became law on February 24, 1863. On December 29, 1863, inaugural ceremonies were held by Governor John C. Goodwin and his territorial officers after they had crossed what they believed was a safe distance into the territory. Governor Goodwin proclaimed that *...the seat of government will for the present be at or near Fort Whipple.* At that time the Prescott area had approximately 50 residents and 14 log cabins.

Initially, Goodwin had been appointed as first Chief Justice by President Lincoln to serve under the governorship of John A. Gurley. When Gurley died unexpectedly, Goodwin assumed the top office. He and his family arrived in Prescott early in 1864, and Goodwin promptly chose a site near the banks of Granite Creek for the government seat. It was there that men were put to work sawing, notching and chinking logs taken from local ponderosa pine trees. They were carefully placed according to plan, and the splendid new structure that emerged with its shake-shingle roof and glass windows became what is called today the "Governor's Mansion." It is still in the same location today on the grounds of the Sharlot Hall Museum.

Prescott township was officially surveyed in 1864. At the suggestion of Territorial Secretary of State Richard C. McCormick, it was named Prescott after William Hickling Prescott, a noted historian who wrote a book entitled, *The History of the Conquest of Mexico.* Prescott streets were named after important figures in Mexican history such as Cortez, Montezuma, Coronado and Alarcón. Goodwin, Whipple, Walker, Gurley and Sheldon Streets were named after men who were instrumental in the settling and building of Prescott.

In 1864 the first 4th of July celebration was held, starting a tradition that continues today as Prescott's Frontier Days and Rodeo. The first celebration drew over 500 people and was attended by the Governor and soldiers from Fort Whipple. The downtown celebration of band concerts, picnics, and fireworks constituted the traditional family outing. The rodeo was established to give rowdy cowboys a place to let off steam and was first held on July 4, 1888.

The year 1867 brought a period of sadness to Prescott when Margaret Hunt McCormick, young wife of Richard McCormick, died in childbirth on April 30. Their tiny daughter also died, and the two were laid to rest together in a plain coffin. A rose bush brought to Prescott by Margaret still blooms today in front of the Governor's Mansion.

The new town and its surrounding land became a desirable place to homestead, mine gold, establish businesses that would supply the needs of the residents—including the troops stationed at Fort Whipple, raise horses and cattle, and help build the backbone of government that established Prescott as the capital of the Arizona Territory. Prescott rapidly developed into a thriving community that boasted elegance and roughness, culture and baseness, and every kind of goods and services, including gambling, numerous saloons, and brothels.

In 1876, with Reconstruction ending (removal of Federal troops from the South), Prescott lost its status as Capital to Tucson. It regained the honor 10 years later. In 1889, however, the capital was once again relocated--this time to Phoenix where it has remained.

Throughout the tumultuous first years of its existence, Prescott never lost its charm and appeal. With its reputation as a lively settlement that offered beautiful scenery, friendly people, a chance to make a decent living, and excellent eating and drinking establishments, people continued to move into the area and prosper. During the 1870s nearly 80 Chinese became part of Prescott's business community. Military personnel from Fort Whipple patronized the businesses that thrived along Gurley, Montezuma and Cortez streets. Miners and ranchers regularly came to town to pick up supplies and engage in a little recreation.

141

Prescott also boasted a social class that lived in upscale houses and frequented the opera house. By the late 1870s the women of Prescott could shop in any of 14 mercantile stores. One of the best-known was owned by the Goldwater family and located at the intersection of Cortez and Union Streets. Morris Goldwater, uncle of Senator Barry M. Goldwater, was instrumental in bringing in the railroad, headed the committee that commissioned the *William O'Neill Rough Rider Monument*, served as mayor for 22 years, and was a member of the Arizona State Legislature.

Another popular store was the J. I. Gardner store on Cortez and Willis, built in 1890. Today the building houses Murphy's Restaurant and the interior has been restored to turn-of-the-century decor. A third store was The Bashford-Burmister Company at 130 W. Gurley Street directly across from the courthouse, built in 1901. It was one of the largest mercantile emporiums in northern Arizona. The original store burned down in 1900, but its replacement can be visited today as Bashford Courts. The lovely Victorian home owned by the Bashford family currently resides on the grounds of the Sharlot Hall Museum.

In 1881 the following description of Prescott was run in the *Phoenix Gazette*:

...she has been remarked as the "toniest" of the Territorial towns. Situated amid the pines that continually sing to her the saddest yet sweetest songs of nature, nestled among the hills at an elevation so high as to never permit the atmosphere to reach that temperature that makes us lose the starch in our garments as well as the polishing points in our manners and habits, she seems to gather refinement from her surroundings. The true indication of culture—not with an "ah" termination, as in its too, too Boston sense—seems to pervade her streets and permeate her homes. You can see more dignified and courtly gentlemen, stylish and polished young men, fascinating and elegant ladies in Prescott in a day, than in any other town of the same size...

In 1878 another famous gentleman came to Prescott, John Charles Frémont, the world-famous cartographer who was instrumental in mapping the West. He had been appointed as Arizona's fifth governor, and was accompanied by his lovely wife Jessie and daughter Lily. A house in which they lived is now located on the grounds of the Sharlot Hall Museum.

In 1878 a new brick courthouse was constructed that was complete with trees, grass, and a fence to keep out wayward horses and cattle. It also had a bandstand, working fountain and electric lights. In 1883 Prescott officially became a city that boasted of two schools, a theater, a concert hall, five churches, 18 saloons and three newspapers. The *Daily Courier* has been the main source of local news from 1881 to today.

Stage coaches ran north and south to connect with the Atlantic and Pacific Railroad. The town's population of 1,836 made it second in size only to Tucson, which boasted 6,994 (census of 1880). When the railroad came to Prescott in January 1887, it was a time of great celebrating. Almost the entire population showed up to greet the long-awaited locomotives that steamed into town after completing a 74-mile run from Seligman. The man who financed this first rail effort, Thomas Bullock, lost the railroad to taxes in 1893, but the Santa Fe, Prescott and Phoenix Railroad came in and took over. Its depot on Sheldon Street is currently still in use as an office building and is a part of the Depot Marketplace.

This was about the time that Buckey O'Neill came to town. A charming and handsome young man, Buckey quickly became part of Prescott's business and social scene. He enjoyed living in Prescott, and expressed his feelings in his cattlemen's newspaper called the *Hoof and Horn*:

...If pure air there be, it is here...The step grows elastic and one feels as though he had drunk of the fabulous fountain of eternal youth.

Buckey has since been immortalized in the famous Solon Borglum bronze statue that stands on front of the historic courthouse. Further information on Buckey O'Neill can be found in this section under *Biographies*.

Prescott's notorious Whiskey Row, now confined to south Montezuma Street between Gurley and Goodwin, early-on extended back to Granite Street (Block 13) and north to Sheldon Street. Its wooden buildings, many of which were little more than shacks, were prone to fire. In early 1883 a saloon fire resulted in significant damage to Row buildings. In July 1890 another fire that started in a miner's shack on the Row burned down a bank, hotel, shops, and other dwellings. November 1890 brought a different kind of disaster when a sawmill boiler exploded and killed six men. The fire that had the biggest impact on downtown Prescott, however, was the great Prescott fire of 1900.

It was about 10:45 pm on Saturday night, July 14, 1900, and the town was sweltering in summer heat that was accompanied by a long period of drought. Whiskey Row was packed with cowboys, miners, bar girls, and assorted local folk out to have a good time. While the pianos played and the sound of laughter echoed up and down the street, a miner staying in an upstairs room of the OK Annex on the southwest corner of Montezuma and Goodwin lit a candle mounted on a miner's candle-pick and stuck it into the wall. When he later went out he left the candle burning and, although no one knows for sure, the flame either ignited loose wallpaper or fell to the floor and set the carpeting on fire. In any case, it was the beginning of a blaze that would destroy all of Whiskey Row and a good part of the downtown.

By 11:00 pm the hotel was an inferno. Someone began to desperately ring the alarm bell, calling the volunteer fire department. Water was in short supply, however, as the reservoir was nearly dry and the pumping station temporarily shut down. There wasn't enough water or pressure to challenge the fire. The flames quickly spread to the roof of the corner brick building and jumped Goodwin Street. As

Scopel Block, Montezuma and Goodwin, c. 1900.
(Sharlot Hall Museum, Prescott, Arizona)

the wind blew from the south, the fire was fueled by the dry wood buildings of Whiskey Row. Some structures were dynamited to try to halt the fire, but building after building ignited and swiftly burned to the ground. Before the flames consumed everything, however, patrons on Whiskey Row were quick to respond. A group of men picked up the 12-foot-long mahogany bar in the Palace saloon and carried it across the street to Courthouse Square where it was put back into business. Liquor, gambling devices, furniture, groceries, display cases, and even a piano were brought to safety while the fire raged.

The great fire ravaged Montezuma, Gurley and North Cortez and Granite streets, destroying over 80 businesses and 60 homes. It also burned much of Willis and Granite Streets but was stopped short of reaching the railroad yards on Sheldon Street.

People came from miles around to watch the flames that lit up the night sky. Folks in Jerome learned about the fire by telephone and made the long journey to Prescott to witness the conflagration. People in Phoenix quickly purchased train tickets to make the trip. By morning there was little left of the downtown except for smoldering piles of rubble, a few brick walls, and tired patrons sleeping in Courthouse Square.

Losses were estimated at between one and two million dollars (about sixty million in today's dollars). Few business or home owners had insurance. Several people were injured, but fortunately no one was killed. One of the few facades left partially standing, that of the Palace Hotel and Bar, gave rise to today's recently restored Palace Restaurant. The famous mahogany bar, little worse for wear, once again stands ready to serve patrons.

Remains of Whiskey Row and tent city in Courthouse Plaza.
(Sharlot Hall Museum, Prescott, Arizona)

Bashford-Burmister building on Gurley Street
(now Bashford Courts) after the big fire.
(Sharlot Hall Museum, Prescott, Arizona)

View of Gurley Street from top of courthouse
after the wall pictured above had been razed.
(Sharlot Hall Museum, Prescott, Arizona)

147

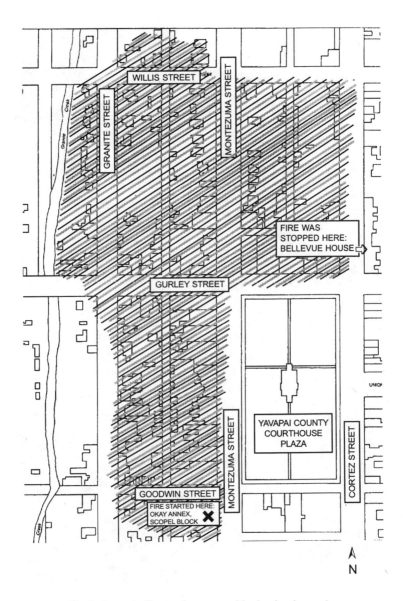

Shaded area indicates downtown blocks that burned.
(Sharlot Hall Museum, Prescott, Arizona)

Today's Hotel St. Michael, rebuilt in 1901 as the Hotel Burke, retains much of the historic interior that impressed patrons such as Teddy Roosevelt, Will Rogers, Tom Mix, and John L. Sullivan. Most of downtown Prescott was rebuilt in 1901 and 1902, and many of those buildings remain today. A list of historic buildings can be found at the end of this section.

Gambling in Prescott flourished until 1907 when it was outlawed. Other kinds of entertainment were brought in to titillate the patrons on Whiskey Row, including the famous belly dancer named "Little Egypt."

The 1900s brought many changes to Prescott. Streets were widened and paved, new buildings were put up, and a certain amount of sophistication crept into the once notoriously wild- west atmosphere that epitomized the town.

The Elks Theater on Gurley Street flourished as a movie theater and opera house. Ladies dressed in the latest fashions strolled the streets with their equally fashionable husbands or beaus.

In 1911 the state-supported Arizona Pioneers Home opened to welcome its first residents. Still functioning today for the same purpose, this haven for disabled miners and pioneer residents of Arizona who have lived in the state for 30 years or more overlooks the city from a high hill and can be seen to the west from the corner of Goodwin and Montezuma.

On February 14, 1912, Arizona become the 48th state to enter the Union. At 12:00 noon a celebration was held in Courthouse Square complete with band music, ringing bells and blowing whistles. Suffragettes campaigned for the right of women to vote, and in 1914 Ms. Fannie Munds was elected the first female state senator in Arizona and only the second in the entire nation.

When World War I began in 1914, Arizona copper was high in demand. In 1917 Prescott formed a military unit that paraded in front of the new courthouse. When the war ended in 1918, Prescott citizens celebrated with a parade around the square. Many veterans who had suffered from poisonous gas in Europe were brought to Fort Whipple for treatment.

In 1916 the elegant courthouse that stands today in the heart of Prescott was begun. The original plans drawn up by an architect called for a more elaborate building topped with a copper dome. The town officials and residents were appalled at the design and projected cost, so a modified version was built. The structure was completed in 1918. In front of the courthouse imbedded in the concrete walkway is a historic timeline that portrays Prescott's historical events interwoven with world events. A second timeline can be found in front of the public library at Marina and Goodwin.

Numerous people moved to Prescott for health reasons. The air and altitude helped asthma and tuberculosis sufferers experience relief. The railroad brought in new residents and encouraged visitors from the East to see Arizona with its many natural wonders.

Automobiles finally rolled into town, although early models had difficulty making it up the steep grades.

In 1913 the first Northern Arizona State Fair was held in Prescott. Aviation stunts were performed, and Tom Mix brought his Wild West show to town. In 1947 the name Northern Arizona State Fair was changed to Yavapai County Fair, and today it is held at the new fairgrounds in Prescott Valley. The rodeo takes place during 4th of July week at the old fairgrounds in Prescott, and horse-racing is run during the summer at the same track.

Movie-makers came to Arizona to partake of the beautiful scenery and use the scenic rock formations, hills and mountains as backgrounds for early westerns. Tom Mix was one of the first to make movies in the Prescott area with his famous steed, Tony the Wonder Horse. He liked Prescott so much that he bought a ranch that he named the Bar-Circle-A. It was located where the Yavapai

Hills residential area and Ramada Inn are today. More recently, much of *How the West Was Won* was filmed in Prescott in 1961. Other movies at least partially made in the Prescott area include *Billy Jack* with Tom Laughlin; *Junior Bonner* with Steve McQueen, Ida Lupino and Robert Preston; *Wanda Nevada* with Brook Shields and Peter Fonda; *Creep Show II; Nobody's Fool* with Rosanna Arquette and Eric Roberts; *The Getaway* with Alec Baldwin and Kim Basinger; *National Lampoon's Vacation* with Chevy Chase; *Universal Soldier* with Jean-Claude VanDamme and Dolph Lundgren; and the made-for-TV movie *Living a Lie* with Peter Coyote and Jill Elkenberry.

As the 20th Century progressed, Prescott evolved into the city it is today. Its borders expanded out in every direction, and Prescott became part of a tri-city area that includes Prescott Valley and Chino Valley. Prescott is also home to several beautiful lakes, including Watson and Willow Lakes, Lynx Lake, and Goldwater Lake.

Libraries and education arrived, including three major schools of higher learning: Embry-Riddle Aeronautical University, Prescott College, and Yavapai College. A full-service airport, Ernest A. Love Field, was dedicated in 1928. The railroad left town, however, running its last train in 1962.

Major shopping areas were built, along with new hotels, restaurants, stores and businesses. The Prescott Community Hospital opened in 1943 (now the Yavapai Regional Medical Center). Fort Whipple was designated as a Veterans Administration Hospital in 1922. Gambling returned in a big way, but not to Whiskey Row. The Prescott Yavapai Indian Tribe built a casino named "Bucky's" in the Prescott Resort and another across Highway 69 from the resort called the Yavapai Casino.

The Sharlot Hall Museum was established in 1928; The Smoki Museum opened in 1935; and the Phippen Museum, founded in 1974, moved to its present location in 1984. The new Fort Whipple Interpretive Center plans to open its doors in the late 2001 as a satellite of the Sharlot Hall Museum.

Entertainment has always been a big part of the social and artistic scene in Prescott. Today top-name performers appear year-'round at the Yavapai College performance hall, including the Phoenix Symphony. The Prescott Fine Arts Association presents a season of fine theater, and the Arizona Jamboree and its star performers regularly appear in town, especially during the summer and at Christmas time. Summer is always rich in music as a result of Prescott's Bluegrass Festival, the Folk Music Festival at the Sharlot Hall Museum, evening concerts in Courthouse Plaza, and noted performers at Yavapai College. Jazz is also popular in a number of downtown establishments and at the Adult Center, and country and rock music reign supreme on Whiskey Row.

Prescott was officially designated as Arizona's Christmas City in 1989. Every year in December the courthouse and gazebo are festively decorated, and the lighting ceremony brings a large group of townfolk and visitors to the square. The city also features a nighttime light parade and a daytime Christmas parade to delight adults and children alike.

The years have been kind to Prescott, and this charming, historic community only improves with age. The area's many features will continue to attract people who want to enjoy the pine-scented air, beautiful scenery, spirit of the old West, and famous hospitality. It has become known as one of the country's most desirable retirement locations. But one of the most important attractions will continue to be the fascinating and colorful Old West history. Without it Prescott would be just another town.

Looking west on Gurley Street with Thumb Butte in background.

Prescott's historic courthouse and Solon Borglum's
William O'Neill Rough Rider Monument.

HISTORIC BUILDINGS

Prescott has many historic buildings within walking distance of Courthouse Plaza. Walking tour and driving tour guides are available for a modest sum at the Visitors Center, 117 West Goodwin Street. Signs describing important historic sites are strategically located in the downtown area.

Many of Prescott's historic buildings were built after the great fire of July 14, 1900. Original names, addresses, and year of construction are as follows:

Courthouse Plaza
Yavapai County Courthouse, 1916-1918

Cortez Street
Bank of Arizona, 101 So. Cortez, 1900
John C. Herndon House, 246 So. Cortez, early 1900s
Hotel Vendome, 230 So. Cortez, 1920s
Knights of Pythias, 105 So. Cortez, early 1900s
J. I. Gardner Store, 201 No. Cortez, 1890
Fisher Goldwater House, 240 So. Cortez, 1894
John C. Herndon House, 246 So. Cortez, 1893
Masonic Temple, 105 No. Cortez, 1900
New State Theater, 129 No. Cortez, early 1900s
Prescott National Bank, 103 No. Cortez, 1902
Raible Block, 114 No. Cortez, early 1900s
John T. Shull House, 225 So. Cortez, 1880
Edmund E. Wells House, 303 So. Cortez, 1878

Goodwin Street
Federal Courthouse and Post Office, 101 W. Goodwin, 1931
Kenwill Apartments, 121 E. Goodwin, early 1900s
Prescott City Jail and Firehouse, 117 W. Goodwin, 1895

Gurley Street
Bank of Arizona, 101 E. Gurley Street, 1877
Bashford-Burmister Company, 130 W. Gurley, 1901

Gurley Street (continued)

Henry Brinkmeyer House, 605 W. Gurley, 1899
Dr. Warren E. Day Octagon, 212 E. Gurley, 1877
Elk's Theater and Opera House, 119 E. Gurley, 1905
First Congregational Church, 216 E. Gurley, 1904
First Congregational Church Parsonage, 214 E. Gurley, 1899
Gurley St. Bar, 230 W. Gurley, 1901
Hassayampa Inn, 122 E. Gurley, 1927
Prescott Public Library (Carnegie Library), 125 E. Gurley, 1903
Washington School, 300 E. Gurley, 1903

Marina Street

Levy House, 147 No. Marina, 1895
Robert Morrison House, 300 So. Marina, 1902
Sacred Heart Catholic Church, 208 No. Marina, 1894-96
Sacred Heart Rectory, 210 No. Marina, 1915
Saint Luke's Episcopal Church, 14 So. Marina, 1892

Montezuma Street

Arizona Hotel (and brothel), 214 So. Montezuma, late 1800s
Brinkmeyer Hotel, 114 No. Montezuma, late 1800s
J.W. Wilson Clothing Company & Wilson Apt., 102 No. Montezuma, early 1900s
Levy Building, 112 So. Montezuma, 1901
Palace Hotel and Bar, 120 So. Montezuma, 1901
Sam'l Hill Hardware, 154 So. Montezuma, 1901
St. Michael Hotel (formerly Hotel Burke), 102 So. Montezuma, 1901

Sheldon Street

Santa Fe, Prescott & Phoenix Railroad Depot, 100 E. Sheldon, 1907

Union Street

C.A. Peter House, 211 E. Union, 1898
Henry Goldwater House, 217 E. Union, 1894
Jake Marks House, 203 E. Union, 1894
Lawler-Hetherington Double House, 225 E. Union, 1894

VICTORIAN HOMES

Beautiful Victorian-style homes can be found on Mount Vernon, Park, North Grove, South Cortez, West Gurley, Alarcon, Pleasant, and other streets in the downtown area. In addition to the houses mentioned in the *Historic Buildings* section, a number of these picturesque structures and the names of their early owners are as follows:

Alarcon Street
W. A. Cline House, 229 So. Alarcon, 1890s

Grove Street
Arthur Robinson House, 115 No. Grove, 1899

Mt. Vernon Street
A. Blumberg House, 145 No. Mt. Vernon, 1900
John J. Hawkins House, 122 So. Mt. Vernon, 1895
Hazeltine House, 202 So. Mt. Vernon, 1903
O. A. Hesla House, 141 So. Mt. Vernon, 1898
Morin House, 134 No. Mt. Vernon, 1899
John H. Robinson House, 204 No. Mt. Vernon, 1900
C. A. Sewell House, 220 No. Mt. Vernon, 1893
Governor Richard E. Sloan House, 128 No. Mt. Vernon, 1900
W. H. Timerhoff House, 116 So. Mt. Vernon, 1899
Dr. J. R. Wall House, 146 So. Mt. Vernon, 1901

Park Street
Amy Hill House, 144 So. Park, 1906

Pleasant Street
E. P. Clarke House, 109 No. Pleasant, late 1800s
Fredericks House, 203 So. Pleasant, 1902
J. C. Martin House, 125 No. Pleasant, 1890
T. W. Otis House, 113 No. Pleasant, 1877

CEMETERIES

Prescott has fourteen known cemeteries that date back to the town's very beginning. A few are small, private burial grounds; nine are accessible to the public. Visitors are requested to protect the fragility of these historic grounds.

Arizona Pioneers' Home Cemetery and Simmons Cemetery

The Arizona Pioneers' Home Cemetery is located on Iron Springs Road in the Miller Valley area of Prescott, just east of the Ponderosa Plaza Mall. Its first burial was held in 1972.

Next to it on top of the hill is the old Simmons Cemetery (also known as the Pioneers' graveyard, Ritter Cemetery and Miller Valley Cemetery) that had its first burial in 1911, although there may have been earlier burials. Prescott historian Sharlot Hall and artist Kate Cory are buried here, along with Sharlot's parents. Doc Holiday's lady-friend "big-nosed Kate" is reported to be buried here.

During the years that Sharlot Hall was involved with documenting the lives of Yavapai County pioneers, she became interested in caring for the resting place of those buried in what was then known as the Pioneers' graveyard. She had an old fence repaired to keep out wandering livestock, and had accumulated trash and weeds removed. She had trenches dug to carry away the rain and melting snow, and arranged for rock terraces. She also drew up a map of the graves and took over caring for the adjoining Miller Valley graveyard. When Sharlot was 12 years old and traveled west with her family on the old Santa Fe Trail, she would stop and erect small headboards on forgotten graves along the way. Later in life she resolved to find the remains of Yavapai County pioneers who were buried in remote and uncared-for places and move them to Prescott cemeteries.

Grave markers of Sharlot Hall (left) and Kate Cory (right).
Center stone marks the grave of Sharlot's parents.

Citizens Cemetery

Citizens Cemetery is a very old, picturesque cemetery located at 815
East Sheldon Street, behind the Smoki Museum. Previously known
as the Town Cemetery, Prescott Cemetery, City Cemetery, County
Cemetery and Citizens Burying Ground, this 6.5-acre plot of land
had its first burial in 1864. The last interment occurred in 1933
except for later burials for those who had reserved a plot. Over
2,500 persons from all walks of life are buried here, including
veterans from two World Wars, the Civil War, the war with Mexico,
the Indian Wars, and the Spanish-American War. One corner of the
cemetery contains graves of Chinese residents who lived and died in
Prescott in the late 1800s and early 1900s.

In an unmarked grave in the potter's field section of the cemetery
lies Jim Parker, who in 1897 was hung in Courthouse Plaza after
having led a life of cattle rustling, train robbery and murder. He
killed a deputy district attorney in 1897 and was sentenced to death
by hanging. Sheriff George Ruffner released the trap-door.

Citizens Cemetery was listed in the National Register of Historic Places in 1994 and is part of the Prescott Armory Historic Preservation District. This burial ground is in the process of being restored. A new front wall, iron fence and entryway have recently been added. Prescott area residents have the opportunity to assume responsibility for caring for a pioneer gravesite, and will be given information on the person buried there. Further information about Citizens Cemetery can be obtained by writing to the Yavapai Cemetery Association, 201 South Pleasant Street, Prescott AZ 86303, or calling 520/778-5988.

Entrance to Citizens Cemetery.

I.O.O.F. Cemetery

The Independent Order of Odd Fellows Cemetery is located at 400 South Virginia Street. Its first burial was in 1890, and originally it was co-owned with the Knights of Pythias. Still receiving interments, it is now operated by the Mountain View Cemetery of Prescott.

Masonic Cemetery

Near the center of town is the small Masonic Cemetery, one of the oldest in Prescott. It was first used in the late 1860s, and is located on Carondolet between Sheldon and Gurley. It is home to approximately 350 gravesites and is still being used for burials today. Town father Morris Goldwater is buried here. This cemetery is not open to the public except by appointment. Call 717-0527 for further information.

Mountain View Cemetery

Mountain View Cemetery, located at 1051 Willow Creek Road, is a still-active place of burial that conducted its first interment in 1910. It currently contains over eleven thousand graves and a privately owned mausoleum. Mountain View was established by the Ruffner family, who still offers funeral services in the Prescott area today. The story goes that Sheriff George Ruffner, who presided at the time of Prescott's great fire in 1900, won an undertaking parlor during a game of faro in the Palace Saloon in 1903. George's younger brother eventually took over the business, and it has remained in the family ever since (see *Edmund E. Wells House* in the *Historic Buildings* section).

Prescott National Cemetery

The Prescott National Cemetery is located at the junction of Highways 69 and 89, and can be reached by turning right off Highway 89 just after it turns north. Its first recorded interment was in 1888, although records indicate that 145 people were buried here before then. Its last burial was in 1974. Laid to rest in this cemetery are veterans of the Civil War, Indian Wars, Spanish-American War, World War I, World War II, Korean Conflict and Vietnam Conflict. Some civilians including Indian scouts and spouses of interred veterans are also buried here.

Entrance to Prescott National Cemetery.

Rolling Hills Cemetery

A little-known cemetery lies in northeast Prescott between the airport and the Antelope Hills Golf Course. Ruger Road divides it in two. This small plot of land first known as Granite View Cemetery was used for interments in the 1930s (during the Great Depression). Opened by the Ruffner family as a moderately priced burial ground, it was sometimes used as a paupers' field. Most burials occurred between 1933 and 1950. Like the Citizens Cemetery, it is home to the remains of many Chinese immigrants. This cemetery was never surveyed or platted, so there is no accurate recording of burial sites. Some graves may still reside under the golf course. It is estimated that over 500 people are resting in this forlorn little piece of property. Recent efforts have been made to clean up the site and restore some dignity to this remote burial ground.

Yavapai County Cemetery

This early burial ground is situated behind recently constructed medical buildings on Ainsworth, behind a fence and adjacent to the Mountain View Cemetery. Originally located where the Prescott High School athletic fields and gymnasium are now, this small cemetery is home to a mass grave containing the remains of approximately 845 people. The graves were unearthed and relocated in 1958-59 before the high school was built. A large round rock cistern can be found on the grounds.

Yavapai-Prescott Indian Tribe Cemetery

A small cemetery reserved for members of the Yavapai-Prescott Indian Tribe is located on the reservation.

Yavapai woman outside wikiup, c. 1900.
(Sharlot Hall Museum, Prescott, Arizona)

THE YAVAPAI-PRESCOTT
NATIVE AMERICAN INDIANS

The Yavapai Native American Indians who live on the Yavapai Reservation adjoining the city of Prescott do not trace their heritage to nomadic tribes. Their oral tradition is that the Yavapai have always been in the Southwest. Current archaeological research, however, indicates that the Yavapai arrived as early as the year 1000 and as late as the 1500s. Many tribes evolved from the original people, and the Yavapai are part of the Yuman language-speaking group who traveled on foot in small parties made up of extended families. The name Yavapai, means "people of the sun." For hundreds of years they lived on the land, trading with other tribes, unaware of amazing events that were occurring beyond the mountains and deserts of the Southwest. One day in the late 1500s they were startled by an amazing sight: white men on horseback wearing strange-looking clothing making their way through the mountains and across the deserts.

From 1583-1604 four different expeditions of Spanish soldiers and missionaries came up from Mexico and traveled through the Southwest exploring the terrain and searching for gold. They were greeted by American Indians, sometimes in a friendly manner and other times with hostility. Diaries from these expeditions mention the Yavapai people as being friendly. A map drawn by Catholic priest Father Pedro Font indicated the presence of Yavapai and Hualapai Indians west of the Agua Fria and Gila Rivers, and east of the Colorado River.

In the late 1700s and early 1800s the Native American people of the Southwest regularly came face-to-face with explorers and missionaries, mountain men (trappers and prospectors), U.S. Army soldiers, and settlers. Most natives did not take kindly to the invasion of their lands. In Arizona the Athabascan-speaking Apache warriors went on raids against the white man, resulting in great battles with the military that left many dead on both sides. The Yavapai and

Hualapai often joined the Apaches and as a result had their ranks decimated. Prior to 1865 the Yavapai tribe numbered approximately 6,000 (tribal estimates go as high as 10,000). By 1875 their numbers had dwindled to less than 1,500. By 1900 only about 400 were still alive.

During the early days of the West terrible battles raged between the white men and red men. Miners and settlers wanted land for farming, ranching and mining. The indigenous people fought to keep their homeland and hunting grounds. Some white men tried to keep peace between the two, including one of the first men in the Prescott area, prospector Pauline Weaver. Claiming to be half Cherokee, Pauline was friendly with the local Yavapai, but ironically was accidentally shot by one of the braves in June 1865. He never really recovered from these wounds and died at Camp Lincoln on June 21, 1867.

Atrocities occurred. In 1864 the Yavapai and Pinal Mountain Apaches were invited to a "peace feast" where their food was poisoned. Thirty-six Indians died at the hands of local people. The host group included Prescott residents. This tragedy is known as the Pinole Massacre and is also called the Incident at Bloody Tanks. In 1866, 30 Yavapai were killed and 40 wounded by soldiers at an ambush in a place called Skull Valley on August 13, 1866.

Many people confused the Yavapai Indians with the Apache because they wore similar dress and had similar physical appearance. In fact, the Yavapai were not extremely hostile to the white man and often tried to coexist peacefully. The Yavapai also had a good relationship with the Apaches and in many cases men and women from the two tribes intermarried.

In 1864 the U.S. Army requested Government money to establish reservations for Indians that would be based around military forts. The Indians were told that these camps would be a safe place to live, and that they would be housed, fed, and given horses. Most of those who accepted the offer were not treated well, however, and left to go back to their former homes. Many Indians contracted small pox or malaria in the camps and died.

The Apaches and Yavapai who fought the invaders attacked military wagon trains and stagecoaches, burned ranches, and stole horses and cattle. Armed with rifles, they reduced the number of U.S. military in the area significantly. Morale became low among the soldiers, and many left after their tour of duty was up. More and more private citizens began going after the Indians. Attacks increased. By 1870 the Army was fed up with the situation and decided to send in a new general named Ord who believed the Indians should be removed by whatever means possible.

More soldiers were sent to Arizona. The Army began a large-scale effort to round up the Native Americans and put them on reservations. By then there was no difference between the Apaches and Yavapai as far as the Army was concerned. The objective was to take control of the situation and maintain order. In 1871 General George Crook was brought in to resolve the problem (see *Histories and Biographies* section on Fort Whipple). This was the beginning of the end of freedom for the Native American Indians of the Southwest.

In December 1872 over 100 Yavapai men, women and children were killed by soldiers in the Skeleton Cave conflict near Fort McDowell. The Yavapai were being worn down and becoming desperate. In April 1873 close to 2,300 surrendered to General Crook at Camp Verde.

The U.S. Army had difficulty providing for the thousands of Indian people on reservations. Men, women and children had to be housed and fed and it was impossible to keep track of everyone. Apache and Yavapai braves regularly escaped and went on warring parties in Arizona and into Mexico. Soldiers chased after them and especially tried numerous times to capture famed Apache Geronimo. By 1874 most members of the Apache, Yavapai and Hualapai tribes, including 1,500 Yavapai, had been rounded up and brought to the Rio Verde Agency.

In February 1875 the U.S. Government imposed an incredible hardship on the Native American people. In accordance with a Congressional order, the U.S. Army was forced to move the Fort Verde camp inhabitants to the San Carlos Apache Reservation. These poor souls walked a distance of over 175 miles through harsh terrain of rock, brush and cactus, in the middle of winter, with little food or water. They were not allowed to use established roads, but rather were taken over rough trails that led east to East Verde, then south to Rye and Globe, and finally to San Carlos. Everything the Indians owned they carried on their backs. Their moccasins wore out and their feet bled. Many died along the way from lack of food, exhaustion, and injuries caused by the brutal conditions. Bodies were left along the trail as there was no time for burial. Many drowned during difficult creek and river crossings. Babies born on the march froze to death. The 15 soldiers accompanying the sad procession helped carry children and old people across rushing water on their horses or threw ropes to those in danger of being swept downstream. One U.S. Army doctor had volunteered to accompany the Indians. This terrible journey was called the "March of Tears" and claimed the lives of approximately 115 Yavapai men, women and children.

Twenty-five years later, only 200 of the original 1,500 Yavapai who made the trek remained. During the years on the San Carlos Apache Reservation numerous members of the tribe died of disease. The Yavapai and Apache did not get along and wanted only to leave. Unscrupulous Indian agents made the situation worse. Eventually many of the Yavapai people simply walked away from San Carlos and made their way back to their original lands. They found jobs in the mines or worked for white families. Others lived as they could near the Army forts. Most of them ended up in Camp Verde, Arlington (east of Phoenix), Fort McDowell (west of Phoenix), and Prescott. Today the Yavapai are mainly to be found on the Fort

McDowell and Prescott Reservations, with others living in or near Camp Verde and Clarkdale.

Porch of J. I. Gardner Building, looking southwest, c. 1895.
(Sharlot Hall Museum, Prescott, Arizona)

Note: Building today (201 North Cortez) is Murphy's Restaurant.

Two of the most beloved of the Prescott Yavapai were a talented woman named Viola Jimulla and her husband Sam (see "Viola" in the *Sculptures* section). Viola was born in 1878 in the mountains east of Fort McDowell to parents who had both made the March of Tears. Her father died when she was small, and her mother remarried a Yavapai man named Pelhame who had been a U.S. Army scout. The family worked hard and did well. Viola attended school first at the Rice Indian School, and then at the Phoenix Indian School where she excelled. During the summers and on weekends she worked at odd jobs to earn extra money and gain some sense of independence. When she was 21 she visited her mother and stepfather who had moved to the Fort Whipple area to be near family members. After seeing the high desert and beautiful pine trees, she decided to leave Phoenix and move north.

Viola soon found a job as a cook, working for the boss of the Blue Bell Mine (her stepfather was working in the mines in Mayer). Active and enthusiastic about life, she enjoyed exploring the area. She made many friends, especially among the young Yavapai men and women. In the summer of 1900 she took a train to downtown Prescott for the 4th of July celebration. There she met the shy Sam Jimulla, a young Yavapai man who was to become her husband. They were married in Prescott in 1901 when Viola was 23 years old.

Viola and Sam had a successful and loving marriage. Together they produced five daughters, two of whom unfortunately died in infancy. When the three remaining daughters became old enough, they were sent to the Phoenix Indian School because Sam and Viola believed that a good education was important. Sam worked in the mines around Prescott and helped his fellow Yavapai in any way he could. The family was well-liked and respected in the community.

In 1922 Viola became a Sunday school superintendent and elder at the Yavapai Indian Mission in Prescott that was run by the Presbyterian Church. Sam worked as an interpreter and teacher.

In 1933 during the Great Depression Sam was put in charge of Indian work crews for the WPA. Houses and community buildings constructed from native stone were built in the Camp Yavapai area. Several of these structures are still being used today.

In 1935 Sam and Viola led an effort to have Camp Yavapai officially designated by the United States Government as an official reservation. A united community front that included historian Sharlot Hall and other prominent Prescottonians helped influence the Government to declare 75 acres that were formerly part of the Fort Whipple Military Reserve as the Prescott Yavapai Indian Reservation. Sam Jimulla was appointed Chief by the Commissioner of Indian Affairs, and members of the tribe also elected him Chief. In 1956 another 1,320 acres were added to the reservation.

Sam was a trusted leader. He worked diligently with his people and the local community. Viola was active in her missionary work and, as a way to earn money for the mission and to finance her church activities, used her skills as an expert basket weaver to design, teach, and produce unique and prized straw baskets. She became famous for her beautiful creations.

The 1940s brought much sadness to Viola. First her daughter Amy died at age 28, then Sam was thrown from his horse three months later and succumbed to his injuries. Viola had little time for grief, however. She had taken in Amy's four children, and now faced the task of raising them by herself with the help of other family members. In addition to this large responsibility, she was designated Chieftess of the Prescott Yavapai.

Viola was a stern but benevolent Chieftess. She remained active in her church, and fought for equal opportunity for the Yavapai people. She worked diligently with the Tribal Council to improve the lives of the Yavapai. Never one to lag behind, she kept up with the times and made sure her people had all modern conveniences and good schools.

Viola was a popular public speaker, especially at Indian gatherings. She served as a court interpreter and as a camp counselor. She loved the land and traveled in the West whenever she could. She especially revered the Prescott area and the Granite Mountains, and the land on which the reservation was situated. She loved her people and her religion, and especially enjoyed working with children. Viola left a legacy that remains strong with the Yavapai people today.

For the rest of her life Viola designed and wove her beautiful baskets. Her reputation as a master weaver spread throughout the West. It was a great loss to the Yavapai people and the Prescott community then when Viola died in 1966. She had lived a memorable and productive 88 years and was posthumously inducted into the Arizona Women's Hall of Fame.

The Prescott Yavapai Indians of today are active in many areas, including their thriving businesses: the luxury Prescott Resort and Conference Center, the Frontier Village Shopping Center, Bucky's Casino, the Yavapai Casino, service station and mini-mart, smoke shop, and the Sun Dog Industrial Park. The Tribe is one of the area's largest employers.

It's been over 125 years since Viola's parents and so many Yavapai were part of the tragic "March of Tears." Since then the Prescott Yavapai have made giant strides forward. They constantly strive to preserve and maintain their culture and heritage while at the same time improving reservation education, health and housing. They continue to work for the good of their community and the Prescott area by employing the same spirit and fervor that sustained them during the many years of hardship and pain.

Chieftess Viola Jimulla
(Sharlot Hall Museum, Prescott, Arizona)

Solon Borglum amid sculptures in Paris Salon, 1898.
Woman seated at right is his aunt. Fox terrier
belongs to his future wife, Emma Vignal.
(Sharlot Hall Museum, Prescott, Arizona)

SOLON HANNIBAL BORGLUM

Solon Hannibal Borglum (1868-1922) was a famous and talented artist who created a legacy in bronze and marble sculpture, including Prescott's famed *William O'Neill Rough Rider Monument.* Born in Ogden, Utah, Solon moved to Nebraska with his family as a child. There he grew to love the outdoors, nature and animals. His father was a doctor who owned horses. Solon cared for the great animals and, as he grew older, began sketching them. Dr. Borglum took Solon with him as his assistant, and together they attended the sick which included patients of all social classes including the poor plains Indians. Young Solon developed values such as caring, loyalty, and serving mankind regardless of ethnic background.

The Borglum family consisted of five boys and one girl. Gutzon, who was closest in age to Solon, also expressed artistic talent at a young age and preceded his brother in following a life of drawing and sculpture. In later years he would become known world-wide for his monumental creation of Mount Rushmore in South Dakota.

When Solon was in his teens his family moved to California, which gave the young artist first-hand knowledge of the western cowboy and the mighty horses they rode. Enthralled by this lifestyle but longing for the plains of the Midwest, he returned to Nebraska in the 1884-85 timeframe to work on a ranch full-time. There he continued to draw and try to catch the image of the ranch animals as they exhibited their natural wild spirit.

When Solon was 22 years, old his brother Gutzon and his artist wife stopped in Nebraska on their way to Paris. Gutzon had studied art in San Francisco, and when he saw Solon's sketches, he strongly urged him to take art classes. Solon took his advice and began studying in Omaha. After Gutzon and his wife returned from Europe and settled again in San Francisco, Solon joined them for a brief time, working with Gutzon in his art studio. After a while he moved to Los Angeles, then to Orange County where he began to teach art and paint landscapes and portraits. In 1895 at age 27 He was accepted by the Cincinnati Art Academy for a two-year course of study. There he began modeling in clay, specializing in horse figures. These small sculptures were so well executed that by his second year of school he had 17 displayed in the annual exhibition.

In 1897 Solon had the urge to see Europe. He worked his way across the Atlantic on a cattle boat, and finally reached France where he set out for Paris. In those days sculpture was not a popular medium in the United States, but Paris offered so many beautiful statues that Solon could scarcely believe his eyes. He especially admired the magnificent bronzes by Auguste Rodin. Solon visited museums and parks and walked the picturesque streets studying the people and architecture. He sketched animals at the zoo. In a local stables he discovered a beautiful mustang that had been left behind by Buffalo Bill after a European tour and proceeded to draw him.

After several months of watching and learning, Solon rented a large tool shed that he turned into a studio and began sculpting clay models of horses in western tack and saddles. His sculpture *Lassoing Wild Horses* made an impression on the French and captured honors in all exhibits in which it was submitted. By 1898 Solon was doing life-size horse sculptures and became known in Europe as a sculptor of substance.

That same year Solon met a lovely French woman named Emma Vignal whom he married. She was totally supportive of his work and gladly accompanied him to the United States when he decided to return to the plains in 1899 to pursue his art. They visited the Sioux people in South Dakota and lived among them. Europe beckoned once again, however, so in 1900 the young couple returned and Solon entered his impressive life-size bronze entitled *Stampede of Wild Horses* in the Paris Exposition. This extraordinary work dominated the U.S. pavilion and won a silver medal.

As the new century got underway, Solon continued to sculpt outstanding figures on commission. He entered some of his work in exhibits including the 1904 St. Louis World's Fair (Louisiana

Purchase Exposition). One of the pieces is familiar to Prescottonians today: it was a small version of *Cowboy at Rest* that stands at the south end of Courthouse Plaza. The exposition was also was a prize venue for his four life-size groups (including *Stampede of Wild Horses*) that made bronze history.

As Solon moved into larger-than-life bronze sculptures, he received commissions for monumental works. One was an equestrian statue of General John B. Gordon, of the Confederate States Army, to be displayed in Atlanta, Georgia (commissioned in 1905); and another was for the *William O'Neill Rough Rider Monument* which now stands in Prescott's Courthouse Plaza (commissioned in 1906).

The townspeople of Prescott had gathered $10,000 which, in those days, was considered to be a goodly sum of money (approximately $400,000 in today's dollars). A delegation of men from Prescott went east in search of a sculptor, not knowing who they might talk to who would be interested in doing such a piece for a limited sum. Artist Borglum, who usually received much more for an undertaking of such magnitude, heard about the quest of the Prescott men and offered to sculpt the statue for the $10,000. He was willing to do it because of his love of the West and the people and the spirit of the West, and the subject matter of war hero Buckey O'Neill mounted upon a spirited steed. The men were ecstatic when they talked to Borglum and immediately accepted his offer. They could not believe their good fortune. There were no artistic constraints placed upon Borglum's creativity, and the results are visible today in the magnificent Courthouse Plaza bronze.

The artist himself came to Prescott to locate a granite boulder pedestal on which to mount his masterpiece. The one that he chose rested on a nearby hillside and weighed 28 tons. After the statue had been cast at the Roman Bronze Works in New York City, it was crated for shipment by train to Prescott. Although it was misplaced in Albuquerque for a few weeks, it arrived the morning of the planned celebration on July 3, 1907. Borglum was there, and the crowd cheered wildly when the statue was unveiled. It was and is today one of the most beautiful and exciting sculptures ever executed by Borglum. Many believe it is the greatest of all his works. Even Teddy Roosevelt exclaimed in a letter to Borglum:

I like that statue of Bucky O'Neill very much. He was an absolutely fearless and daring man; and it seems to me you have caught his spirit exactly...

Later that same year Solon Borglum and his family moved to Silvermine, Connecticut, where they bought a spread of land they named Rocky Ranch. Borglum set up a studio and continued to work on large pieces. Some of the works coming out of Borglum's later years were the *Jacob Leisler Memorial Monument* erected in New Rochelle in 1913; *The American Pioneer, A Reverie* for the 1915 San Francisco Panama-Pacific Exposition; and a series of five busts of Civil War generals for the Vicksburg National Military Park in Mississippi.

In 1922, at the young age of 53 years, Solon Borglum became extremely ill from a ruptured appendix which resulted in his death. He had been a devout family man, a community leader, and a great artist. He founded The School of American Sculpture in New York, and was revered as a teacher. But for many he will be most remembered for his brilliant bronzes, among them being one of the most detailed and electrifying: that of Buckey O'Neill astride a magnificent horse. Not a day goes by without someone standing in front of this grand figure and pondering the fate of Captain O'Neill and the brave and colorful Rough Riders.

Small Borglum bronze *Evening,* c. 1904,
exhibited in Prescott Valley Civic Center.

Mary Colter, age 23, during her teaching
years in St. Paul, Minnesota.
(The Mary Colter Collection, Grand Canyon National Park)
(Image No. 16950)

MARY ELIZABETH JANE COLTER

When the railroad came west, it changed the whole makeup of the wild, unspoiled territory called Arizona. Travelers eager to view such wonders as the Grand Canyon, boarded trains belonging to the Santa Fe Railway as early as 1870, creating the need for lodging and dining along the way. It was this need that gave birth to the Fred Harvey Company and its chain of facilities that included hotels, restaurants, and gift shops. One of the most noted locations for Fred Harvey hotels and the famous black-and-white-uniformed Harvey Girls who worked there, was the South Rim of the Grand Canyon. Even today, travelers can be housed and dined in the very same buildings that served the public so long ago.

During the time that Fred Harvey, an Englishman, was creating his empire in Arizona and the Southwest, a young woman of enormous talent was coming into her prime: Mary Elizabeth Colter. Born in Pittsburgh in 1869, Mary developed an interest in the Southwest early in life. As a young woman she attended the California School of Design in San Francisco. There she became well-acquainted with the style of the Spanish hacienda, the art of the Navajo, Hopi and Zuni people, and the color and music that evolved into her own unique style of architecture and design.

After graduating from design school in 1890, Colter taught drawing and architecture first in Menomenie, Wisconsin, then in St. Paul, Minnesota. At 23 years of age she began a teaching career at Mechanic Arts High School in St. Paul, where she taught an all-male student body. When on vacation in San Francisco one summer, she told a friend that she knew of the facilities being built by Fred Harvey in the Southwest, and expressed a wishful desire to work for him. Although Fred Harvey died in 1901, his sons—who took over the Fred Harvey Company—offered the very surprised Mary a job. In 1902 she received a commission to design the interior of the new Alvarado Hotel in Albuquerque, New Mexico (torn down in 1970).

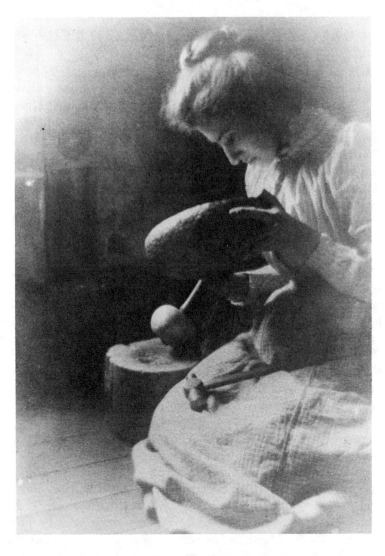

Mary at age 23, working on a pottery piece.
(The Mary Colter Collection, Grand Canyon National Park)
(Image No. 16952)

When Mary Colter joined the Fred Harvey Company, the railroads were experiencing great prosperity: lodging, eating and souvenir offerings along the train routes were much in demand. The men who ran the Harvey Company saw the opportunity to fulfill the needs of the traveling public with buildings that reflected the true flavor of the Southwest. The Native American people who lived near the train stops were famous for their beautifully crafted pottery, jewelry, baskets and blankets. It made sense, then, to bring the two together in a mutually profitable venture that would incorporate gracious buildings, first-class restaurants, and stores that sold fine locally crafted goods. This is where Mary Jane Colter came into the picture with her background, talent and education.

Mary was not only a talented artist, but also a true pioneer--one of the first female architects to be accredited to work in her chosen field. In her pursuit of the Native American style of construction, culture and lifestyle, she visited numerous archeological sites and earned the confidence of local artists and artisans. She collected American Indian jewelry, baskets and pottery. As she developed her expertise in the Southwest arts, she became known as someone who could contribute to the world of local decor in grand style.

In 1904 the Fred Harvey Company hired Mary to design a building in the Native American style that would be located across from the new El Tovar hotel in Grand Canyon Village.

She based her design on Arizona Hopi dwellings, and used Hopi builders to construct the stone and wood building. The new structure, called Hopi House, featured rough plaster walls and ceilings with log beams. Navajo rugs covered the floors, and museum pieces were displayed that eventually became the Fred Harvey Fine Arts Collection. Indian artisans made jewelry, baskets, kachinas and other goods to be sold to visitors. Hopi House is still a beautiful, intact structure today and continues to be a venue for Native American art, jewelry, Kachinas, and other unique items.

Because of the success of her Alvarado Hotel and Hopi House commissions, Mary Colter's reputation grew. In 1910 the Fred Harvey Company offered her a full-time position, that of designing and decorating Harvey hotels throughout the Southwest. Mary's sense of color and taste combined with her love of Native American culture and design made her an excellent choice for a job in a field that few women were hired to work at that time.

Mary was not bashful. Strong-minded, a perfectionist and determined, she nevertheless knew how to work with the male-dominated chain of command that ruled the railroad and hotel companies. A grandson of Fred Harvey said of her:

She was discreet and knew how to get her way. She was an honest, fine person.

Mary Colter's talent was instrumental in shaping the image of the Fred Harvey Company's buildings in the gracious and accurate styling that reflected the Southwest and Native American culture. She drew floor plans and elevations. She developed a coordinated interior and exterior design that often expressed itself as Spanish-Pueblo. She did the interior decor of the El Ortiz Hotel in Lamy, New Mexico (torn down in 1943). She designed the Hermits Rest tourist stop in the Grand Canyon. She then went on to create a scenic structure called the Lookout (Studio) also in the Grand Canyon. Both were done in a rustic stone style and still exist today.

In 1920 plans were laid for Phantom Ranch at the bottom of the Grand Canyon. Mary designed the buildings and did the interior decor. To this day adventurous souls who journey to the bottom of the canyon will stay in the same buildings.

Ms. Colter also designed the El Navajo hotel in Gallup, New Mexico (torn down in 1957). The El Navajo was her tribute to Native Americans and was adorned with beautiful sand paintings and Navajo rugs. In 1924 she decorated the Fred Harvey shops and restaurants in Chicago's new Union Terminal. Then she traveled west again—to Santa Fe, New Mexico, where she tackled a remodeling of the famous La Fonda hotel.

The La Fonda was a unique structure built in the Spanish-Pueblo style that had been purchased by the Santa Fe Railway. With its adobe look, terraced roofs and projecting vigas, the hotel featured a large open courtyard and Spanish-style fountain. Mary Colter did the entire interior in Mexican decor, with each of the 156 rooms having a different look. The hotel reopened in 1929 to loud acclaim. It is still a beautiful operating hotel today that displays Mary's grand fireplace, light fixtures, and murals that she had commissioned.

Mary Colter went on to decorate train stations in St. Louis, Kansas City, Missouri (restaurant and gift shop), and Los Angeles. The Los Angeles train station still offers a glimpse of her talented hand if you peer through windows into the old Harvey House restaurant which is now used for special events only. The decor is still original Colter, designed and installed when she was 70 years old.

In Winslow, Arizona, on Historic Route 66, the La Posada Hotel exhibits Mary's unique sense of Spanish hacienda architecture and decor. Built to present visitors with the experience of staying with a rich landowner and his family in their beautiful home, the hotel retains its historic charm. It is in the process of being authentically restored by new owners. This grand hotel was Colter's favorite project, and she did all the architecture, decor and landscaping. During construction Mary was there every day in the role of overseer and supervisor.

About 20 of La Posada's original 70 rooms are now being used, and the Turquoise Room restaurant is restored and open to the public. The grounds are lovely. One can still step off the train and walk directly into the hotel. Some of the original furniture and wrought iron pieces that Colter installed have been retrieved, and the owners are bringing the buildings and grounds back to their original appearance as much as possible with the help of old photographs. The cost to build the La Posada in 1930 was one million dollars, and close to a second million was spent on landscaping and decor. The cost to stay there today is a modest sum.

Approximately 50 miles east of Winslow near Holbrook in the Petrified Forest National Park is the unique Painted Desert Inn which was built in 1924, redecorated by Mary Colter in 1947, and is now open to visitors as a National Historic Landmark. This building is worth a stop when visiting the Petrified Forest and Painted Desert. Hopi artist Fred Kabotie painted murals of Hopi Indian legends on the inner walls, as commissioned by Colter.

The very impressive structures on the Grand Canyon's South Rim that can be visited today are some of the most important in the legacy left by Mary Colter. The El Tovar Hotel is one of the finest Harvey structures in the Southwest. Although Mary Colter worked on inside decor, her artistic touches have essentially all been replaced. Bright Angel Lodge, however, which was opened in 1935, still proudly displays Mary's "geological" fireplace made from stones collected from layers of the canyon and laid in the same order. The lodge also features a display of Harvey Company memorabilia and a portrait of Colter. On a related note, a cabin once owned by Buckey O'Neill is now a part of the Bright Angel Lodge and is available to visitors for overnight stays.

One of the "must see" Mary Colter creations in Grand Canyon National Park is the 70-foot Watchtower at Desert View. It is located 23 miles east of Grand Canyon Village, and was designed and built by Ms. Colter as a rest stop for park visitors who took tours out of the Village. Completed in 1933, this magnificent structure appears to be an ancient Native American watchtower ruin which, in fact, is exactly what Colter wanted. She patterned the tower after several she had seen in the Southwest, especially those in Canyon de Chelly and the Mesa Verde cliff dwellings. The ground floor is modeled after a prehistoric pueblo. She personally supervised the placement of each of the native stones in the Watchtower, which include genuine petroglyphs, and commissioned Hopi painter Fred Kabotie to do the impressive murals that adorn the inside walls of the Hopi Room. Fred Greer painted the ancient-style drawings found in the upper galleries.

In 1944, at age 75, Mary Colter decided to retire from the Santa Fe Railway. Train traffic had dwindled and automobiles were becoming the main means of travel. She still worked part-time for the Fred Harvey Company, however, taking smaller assignments like redecorating the Painted Desert Inn. In 1948 Mary moved to Santa Fe, where she did one last job for the Fred Harvey Company, that of redecorating La Fonda's cocktail lounge.

After retiring, Mary went through her vast collection of Indian art, pottery, baskets and jewelry. She put pieces on display at various exhibits and wore much of her jewelry. A large part of her collection went to the Mesa Verde Museum in southern Colorado, where parts of it are currently on display at the Far View Visitors Center in Mesa Verde National Park. Her library of books went to the Grand Canyon Community Library, and her Sioux Indian drawings went to the Custer Battlefield National Monument.

In 1958 this amazing woman whose career spanned 46 years died at age 88. She will be remembered for her talent, hard work, and vision of the American Southwest and its indigenous people that provided the inspiration for her design and architecture. Her unusual and unique contributions are available to be studied and admired by those who visit the locations of her work still open to the ever-searching and curious traveler.

Kate J. Cory, distinguished artist and
friend of the Hopi people.
(Sharlot Hall Museum, Prescott, Arizona)

KATE J. CORY

Consummate artist Kate Cory is famous for her paintings and photos of the Hopi people. Although she did not move to Prescott until she was 51 years old, Kate made a lasting impression on the area and her work can be seen in several locations today.

Born in Waukegan, Illinois, in 1861, Kate knew she wanted to be an artist at an early age. As a young women she moved to New York City where she studied art at Cooper Union and the Art Students League.

Little is known about Kate Cory's life between 1880 and 1905, the year she left New York and headed west.

In 1904 Kate met artist Louis Akin in New York. He told her about life with the Hopi people in Arizona, and that he had lived with the Hopis where he was adopted into a clan. He had painted many portraits and scenes of native life which he showed to Kate. She was so enchanted with Akin's stories that she decided to see the West for herself and attempt to meet the Hopis. As it turned out, she was totally accepted by them and welcomed as a friend. For many years she lived in their midst and shared their lives—an honor never before granted to a white woman. She was sensitive to the feelings and culture of the Hopi and treated all members of the community with utmost respect. They allowed her to photograph them, do sketches, and paint them in their native dress.

After Kate left the Hopi community she moved to Prescott where she lived for 46 years. Her paintings and photographs gained world-wide acclaim, and she was asked to participate in many related activities (including consulting on films in California) in relation to her knowledge of the American Indian. She also ventured into other areas including book design, wallpaper design, and even aircraft camouflage.

While living in Prescott Ms. Cory became a close friend of Sharlot Hall, and worked with the Smoki People (a group of local businessmen—see section on the Smoki Museum), helping them authenticate their Hopi-style ceremonials and performances. She participated in designing and furnishing the unique Smoki Museum, thereby helping preserve the ways of the Hopi. She left many of her artistic works to the Museum where they can be seen today.

Kate was active in many local organizations and was known for her work with charitable groups and gifts to the community. She lived a long, productive life until the year 1956, when at age 96 she moved into the Arizona Pioneer Home. She died there in 1958. The *Prescott Courier* wrote that Ms. Cory was

...one of the West's most famed artists and one of the most beloved pioneer citizens...

A truly unique and gifted woman, Kate Cory helped preserve the ways of her adopted people, the Hopi, both in color and black-and-white. Her work is on display in the Smithsonian Institution, Washington, D.C.; the State Capitol Building, Phoenix; the Prescott Public Library; the First Congregational Church on E. Gurley; and the Smoki Museum. The Sharlot Hall Museum also has many of her works but they are not displayed on a permanent basis.

Fireplace painting by Kate Cory
in the Smoki Museum.

Western artist Paul Coze, 1972.
(Kay Coze)

PAUL COZE

Paul Coze, an extraordinarily talented artist, contributed several significant pieces to the Prescott area, including a large mural in the Prescott City Hall Council Chambers, and the accompanying oil portrait of William Hickling Prescott. He also painted an eight-panel mural entitled *Prelude to Modern Prescott* that hangs in the Phippen Museum's conference room. This large piece depicts scenes of early Prescott from 1840 to 1900 (see *Paintings* and *Museums* sections).

Paul Coze had an unusually interesting and varied background. Born in Syria in 1903, his parents undoubtedly contributed to his life's philosophy and career as painter, photographer, anthropologist, writer and designer. His father was of the French titled family Coze de la Cressonniere and his mother was a Russian princess from the family Dabija-Cotromanich that ruled Yugoslavia for 300 years. As a young man Paul attended L'Ecole National des Arts Decoratifs for four years, and was drafted into the French Army after World War I.

Paul was not only a fine artist, but also a world traveler who pursued many goals and worked with people all over the world. He was active in the French Boy Scouts, and eventually became the National Commissioner of the French Boy Scouts and later the Assistant International Commissioner. He wrote several Boy Scout handbooks. After moving to the Southwest he was French Consul for Arizona for 24 years.

In 1928, while living in France, Paul co-authored a book on the American Indians, a people he respected and admired. In order to research and participate in writing *Mouers et Historie des Peaux-Fouges* (Manners and History of the American Indian) he became fluent in English. The book was published in 1928. In 1930 he headed an expedition sponsored by the Paris Museum of Natural History to study Indian culture in North Saskatchewan and Alberta, Canada, which became a study in anthropology. He founded an organization to study the American Indian that presented lectures, films, plays, authentic Indian dances, and roping demonstrations.

After spending many summers living on reservations in Arizona and New Mexico, he was made a member of seven different Native American Indian tribes. He directed hundreds of performances of Indian dances in France, England and Belgium, and in 1936 organized an exhibit of American Indian modern painters for the Musee de L'Homme in Paris. In 1939 he presented the American Indian ballet/drama *Desert Song* for the U.S. Indian School in Phoenix.

Beginning in 1938 Coze lived in the United States, where he was granted United States citizenship while retaining his French citizenship. He became an artist of renown and was given commissions that resulted in major works of art, many of which are still in place today. He worked for the *Arizona Highways* magazine and *National Geographic,* where he wrote and illustrated numerous articles.

One of the largest of Coze's works that can be seen today is the 16x75-foot mural that dominates the lobby of Terminal 2 at Sky Harbor Airport. It is difficult to describe the brilliant colors and wild textures that make up this stunning piece. Its center panel, entitled *Water and Fire,* features a many-hued Phoenix bird sitting atop a date tree. The left panel, *The Earth,* depicts the Native American people, the first white men in Arizona, and the American eagle, among other things. The right panel, *The Air,* shows outstretched hands reaching toward space. Symbols of scientific and commercial endeavors in Phoenix, plus ranching and mining, are depicted. Fifty-two different materials were used in creating this magnificent three-dimension mural, including various minerals and natural substances such as wood and shells. Mosaic pieces from Mexico and Italy were used, along with French glass, feathers and turquoise. Fifteen separate canvases comprise the piece, which was installed in 1962.

Detail from Terminal 2 mural.

In St. Thomas the Apostle Church, 2312 East Campbell Avenue, are two large side altar paintings by the artist, plus 14 Stations of the Cross that were done in a modern style using bright colors. They required years of working with models and sketches. A master of perspective, Coze produced a set of paintings that invites the viewer to fully appreciate and understand this religious event.

The Town and Country Shopping Center on Camelback at 20th Street is home to a 17-foot-high bronze Phoenix bird with stained glass in its wings and body that was created by Coze in 1956. The sculpture has since been painted white and moved from its original high pedestal to its present location in a series of fountains.

More works by Paul Coze that can be seen in Phoenix include the following:

- Veteran's Memorial Coliseum, State Fair Grounds: murals in the main rotunda and above the concession stand.

- St. Mary's High School, 200 West Jefferson Street: 10x20-foot mural in Blaze Hall that was originally displayed in the Phoenix City Hall Council Chambers. Two sculpture and painted pieces over the main entrance.

- First American Title Building, 111 West Monroe Street. Frieze in the lobby.

Paul Coze at work designing the Stations of the Cross
for St. Thomas the Apostle Church in Phoenix.
(Kay Coze)

His work can also been viewed in the following locations:

- Phoenix: Phoenix Art Museum and Heard Museum

- Flagstaff: Museum of Northern Arizona

- Los Angeles: Southwest Museum

- National Monument Museums of Bandalier, Canyon de Chelly, Casa Grande, Mesa Verde, Montezuma Castle, Tonto, Tuzigoot, Walnut Canyon, and Wupatki in Arizona.

Coze died in 1974, but his work lives on. During his lifetime he accomplished many things, not the least of which was being awarded the French *Chevalier la Legion d'Honneur* and *Chevalier de l'Ordre du Merite Touristique*. The city of Prescott is fortunate to have this fine artist's work prominently displayed both in City Hall and the Phippen Museum. It would be a worthy venture to travel the state in search of the art of Paul Coze.

Phoenix Bird Sculpture at Town and
Country Shopping Center.

Sharlot Hall, age 40.
(Sharlot Hall Museum, Prescott, Arizona)

SHARLOT MABRIDTH HALL

The year was 1870 when, in a log cabin on the wind-swept prairies of Lincoln County, Kansas, Sharlot Mabridth Hall made her first appearance. A child of the frontier, Sharlot was just 12 years old when her family (parents, brother Ted, and aunt and uncle) left the hard life they had experienced in Kansas and traveled west by covered wagon, along the Santa Fe Trail to the Arizona Territory. Sharlot rode her mare, following a herd of 20 horses and two wagons. She always remembered this long journey west, especially because she was thrown by her horse, sustaining a spine injury that would plague her for the rest of her life. The three-month journey was long and hard, but Sharlot suffered through it, using it as a springboard from which she would mold her life as a writer and lover of the West and its people.

When the Hall family arrived in the Prescott area in 1882, they settled on lower Lynx Creek in Lonesome Valley (near today's Prescott Valley) where they lived in tents and raised cattle. Sharlot's father also worked at mining placer gold and for a while in a large hydraulic mining operation. Sharlot and her brother helped with chores and attended school in Cherry Creek (today's Dewey) off and on for three years. By the time Sharlot was 13 she had begun to write impressive verse. When she was 16 her teacher recommended that she be sent to Prescott for further schooling. Her parents agreed, and Sharlot boarded in the home of a judge during the week to attend the new Prescott High School, returning to Lonesome Valley on weekends to help out at the ranch.

At age 17 Sharlot left school and returned to her family to help with their mining efforts and to assist her ailing mother who had never fully recovered from the trip west. For three years she looked after the gold her family had taken from the earth, and slept with a gun under her pillow. Three years later, in 1890, her father decided to give up mining and move to a new homestead called Orchard Ranch, located just off what is now Highway 69 in Dewey. Highway 69 was a dirt road from Prescott and Fort Whipple to Camp Verde.

When the Halls decided to plant apple, pear and peach trees to supplement their income, they unearthed some prehistoric Indian artifacts that whetted Sharlot's interest. She began to ride out to search for old ruins in the area and visit ancient cliff dwellings. She found many sites looted of artifacts that had been taken to supply the demand from people living in the east. Sharlot submitted articles about her findings to various magazines, and several were accepted. This small triumph gave her encouragement and an increased hope of one day being a successful writer.

In 1892 Sharlot's earlier back injury flared up. She experienced severe pain and could not sit or stand for an entire year. In trying to be productive during this time, she wrote articles and sent them to newspapers and magazines. A publication called the *Archaeologist* bought her piece about the Verde Valley cliff dwellings, and *The Great Divide* paid her for a poem and short story. Earning money with her writing talent was a significant achievement for a young woman at this time.

As Sharlot's health returned, she resumed her life of hard work on the ranch. Tending cattle, cooking and cleaning took up most of her day, but she still found time to write. One day good fortune came her way when some of her work was accepted and published in a California magazine called *Land of Sunshine*. It literally changed her life. The editor took a special interest in Sharlot and hired her as a staff editor. Other publications such as the *New York Evening Post*, *Atlantic* and *Ladies Home Journal* soon accepted her work.

Because of her new job, Sharlot traveled to California on a regular basis. There she met other authors who wrote for *Land of Sunshine* (later to be called *Out West*) and made a host of new friends. When she returned to Arizona she continued to run Orchard Ranch even as she wrote more poetry about Arizona's past and present, the American Indian, water and agricultural problems, the cattle industry, and cowboys. Aware that many pioneers of Arizona's early years were dying, she interviewed as many as she could, writing down their stories for posterity.

As the new century arrived, Arizona politics heated up and Sharlot became actively involved. In 1907 she began clerking for the Territorial Legislature. In 1909 Governor Richard Sloan appointed her Territorial Historian--the first time any woman held public office in Arizona. As a part of her new job, Sharlot traveled by horse and wagon throughout the Arizona Territory, collecting data and taking photographs. A local guide always accompanied her as she made her way through the rugged land. She often walked alongside the wagon and always carried a gun.

She visited northern Arizona, the Grand Canyon, and Navajo and Hopi reservations. She lectured in southern Arizona and made her way to the eastern borders and up to the northwest "Arizona Strip" (a section of today's Arizona north of the Colorado River that was briefly part of Nevada and also desired by Utah). Sharlot and her guides followed wagon ruts, well-worn roads, and paths where few had gone before. She slept under the stars, ate simple trail food and drank water strong with alkalai. This was work previously unheard of for a single woman, and Sharlot met the challenge head-on.

In 1910, at the urging of her ever-supportive mother, Sharlot published a book of poetry entitled *Cactus and Pine*. This popular volume brought her further recognition.

Shortly after Arizona became a state in 1912, its new governor did away with her job. Disappointed, Sharlot turned to other things. She had signed a contract with a publishing firm to write a history of Arizona, and so traveled north to the Arizona-Utah border to visit some Hopi villages. While there she received word that her mother was critically ill. Rushing back to Prescott, she arrived only a few hours before her mother died. Sharlot was devastated.

She decided to live again at Orchard Ranch and care for her father. Her back pain returned, disabling her for four months. Discouraged, she tried to sell the ranch but couldn't find a buyer. For 10 years Sharlot struggled with the ranch. She felt totally isolated but was unwilling to leave her father, who was becoming senile and verbally abusive. As she made a meager living selling ranch produce and cattle, her back pain continued to plague her.

A group of businessmen from Prescott approached her with a proposition: would she help them develop a program of American Indian ceremonies and dances that they could perform under the guise of their newly formed group called the "Smoki" people.

Sharlot accepted, and with this project was welcomed back into the literary world. Her earlier book of poetry *Cactus and Pine* was reprinted with a few new poems, and she began a series of speaking engagements that took her to various locations in Arizona and back to California. She became active in the Arizona Federation of Women's Clubs. In 1925 she was chosen as the Republican presidential elector from Arizona and went to Washington, D.C. to deliver Arizona's three electoral votes for Calvin Coolidge. While there she met President Coolidge and his wife at the White House, and appeared before Congress in an unusual dress fashioned from copper mesh over blue silk that had been given her by the United Verde Copper Mine Company. (This dress is now on display at the Sharlot Hall Museum.)

Hostess Sharlot Hall pouring tea, c. 1915.
(Sharlot Hall Museum, Prescott, Arizona)

Throughout her adult life Sharlot proved again and again that she had much to contribute to society as an unmarried woman, which was contrary to what was expected of females at that time. Her parents had always hoped Sharlot would marry and give them grandchildren, but she felt strongly that this was not her lot in life. She wrote:

...my father...would much rather have seen me married...and safely chopping stove-wood to keep another farm cook-stove going than to see my name in "Who's Who in America" as the author of a book of verse and the first woman in her state to hold a public office...It puzzled him that I could have brains enough that anyone would pay me real money for the use of them.

...I'm glad, so glad, that God let me be an out-door woman and love the big things. I couldn't be a tame housecat woman and spend big sunny glorious days giving card parties and planning dresses...

In 1925 Sharlot's father died. Sharlot calmly conducted his funeral and buried him on Orchard Ranch, then proceeded to put the property in order and move forward into a life of her own.

In 1927 she bought a Star touring car and moved to Prescott. There she pursued her dream of taking over the old Governor's Mansion and turning it into a museum of Arizona history and artifacts. Prescott's City Council gave her a life's lease on the mansion and grounds. The 63-year-old structure, which was neglected and in a state of disrepair, launched Sharlot on a mission to restore it with the help of local civic groups.

She cleaned the interior of 50 years' dirt and soot, tore down the wallpapered walls to expose the original logs, removed the exterior clapboard siding, and ordered a new shake roof. Her furniture had been brought from Orchard Ranch, and Sharlot moved into the upstairs garret which became her bedroom/workroom. She also had a small kitchen and bathroom installed.

Sharlot moved briefly into the Hotel St. Michael. Then in May 1929 the newly formed Historical Society of Prescott began to aid Sharlot in her efforts. Friends also contributed time and money, which made her life easier. In 1930 electricity was brought in, and curtains, shade and screens were installed. The interior work was completed and townsfolk were invited to tour the refurbished project. The Sharlot Hall Museum was officially established.

By the mid-1930s Sharlot had the joy of seeing her large rock building (which she called the "house of a thousand hands") completed that would be her new home and house museum displays. This was only the beginning of what is today Prescott's pride and joy. Buildings continued to be relocated to the grounds during and after the life of Sharlot Hall, including Old Fort Misery. Much of the work done on the museum was the result of the U.S. Government's Civil Works Administration (CWA), Federal Emergency Relief Administration (FERA), and Works Progress Administration (WPA) projects during the Great Depression.

During the late 1930s and early 1940s Sharlot became a celebrated author and lecturer who traveled extensively to speak about her knowledge of Arizona and read from her poetry collection. She continued to be a prolific writer, although her book *Poems of a Ranch Woman* was not published until after her death. During her lifetime she published over 500 articles, stories and poems, and ten books credit her as author.

Oil portrait of Sharlot Hall by Prescott artist Tony Cocilovo in Sharlot Hall Museum Administration and Exhibit Building. (Tony Cocilovo)

Sharlot, Major Doran (l.) and Allan Doyle (r.), c. 1900.
(Sharlot Hall Museum, Prescott, Arizona)

Sharlot attended to the museum until April 9, 1943, when, at 73, her life abruptly ended. She had suffered from intermittent heart trouble, and spent the last days of her life in the Arizona Pioneers Home, which overlooks her much-loved city. Sharlot lives on today in the magnificent Sharlot Hall Museum where one can view photos and remembrances of her life and enjoy her legacy in collections and exhibits that preserve the history of early Arizona. A caring, feisty lady who refused to conform to many of the norms of her day, she has been and will continue to be Prescott's premier storyteller, historian, and poet laureate.

Captain William O'Neill, an officer and a gentleman.
(Sharlot Hall Museum, Prescott, Arizona)

WILLIAM OWEN "BUCKEY" O'NEILL

Captain William Owen O'Neill, known to lovers of history and the city of Prescott as "Buckey," was a man of many talents and interests who left a legacy in Prescott. He will always be remembered as the man who in 1898 led a contingent of local volunteers to fight as a part of Teddy Roosevelt's Rough Riders in Cuba during the Spanish-American War.

There is much more to this dashing officer and gentleman, however, than meets the eye. Born in St. Louis in 1860 of Irish parents, William O'Neill grew up to be a bright, energetic student who eventually learned typesetting and legal shorthand. He worked as a court reporter in the East but was drawn to the lure of the West and the stories he read about the great "Pathfinder" John Charles Frémont. He was recruited by Frémont's "campaign" to bring professional men to the Arizona Territory. First he took a job as a typesetter in Phoenix, then moved briefly to Tombstone where Wyatt Earp was deputy U.S. Marshall. There Buckey worked as a reporter on the *Epitaph*. After moving to Albuquerque for a short time where he worked as a court stenographer, he arrived in Prescott in 1882. Here he took a job with a small newspaper called the *Arizona Miner*, and worked as a court stenographer for a local judge. Before long he became a familiar figure on Whiskey Row and was enmeshed in the town's political and social structure.

Almost six feet tall, Buckey had dark brown hair, a neat mustache, and charming smile. Between 1882 and 1898 O'Neill served as Prescott's probate judge, sheriff, mayor, and editor of a cattlemen's newspaper called the *Hoof and Horn*. This outgoing gentleman enjoyed playing cards in the Whiskey Row saloons, and was given the nick-name "Buckey" because he regularly "bucked the tiger," or went against the odds when playing faro.

Buckey was captain of the local militia and a volunteer fireman, plus he helped organize the Arizona Territorial National Guard. He was a "man's man" who enjoyed the company of his mining, cattle and military friends, but was extremely shy around women. It was disconcerting, then, when he saw the comely Pauline Marie Schindler at a traveling medicine show. She was the daughter of an Army captain stationed at Fort Whipple, and Buckey was smitten with her. After a six-month courtship they were married, on April 27, 1886, in Prescott's Catholic church. It was said that Pauline played a fine piano while Buckey tried his hand at writing short pieces of fiction. Early the following year the young couple had a son, Buckey O'Neill, Jr., who sadly lived only two weeks. Eleven years later, in 1897, Buckey and Pauline adopted a four-year-old boy named Morris, who became Maurice O'Neill.

Oil painting of Sheriff Buckey O'Neill
by Tony Cocilovo
(Tony Cocilovo)

In early 1898, after the battleship *Maine* was sunk in Havana harbor, President McKinley authorized Arizona Territory Governor Myron McCord to "raise a regiment of cowboys as mounted riflemen." These men were to be known as the First U.S. Volunteer Cavalry under the command of Colonel Leonard Wood. The country was getting ready for war with Spain, which was officially declared on April 25, 1898. Then Assistant Secretary of the Navy, Theodore Roosevelt, took over command on July 1, 1898.

O'Neill, now the mayor of Prescott, was the first to volunteer. Along with a journalist friend named James McClintock and mining engineer and former Army officer Alex Brodie, they set to work recruiting local cowboys. As the recruits began arriving in Prescott, most of them were housed at Fort Whipple, but the hotels also filled up and Whiskey Row saloons were overflowing. When orders came for the men to move out, the Governor gave them a rousing farewell address.

On May 4, 1898, Captains O'Neill, Brodie and McClintock led over 200 charges from Fort Whipple to downtown Prescott. They then proceeded down Montezuma Street to the depot on Sheldon Street, where they boarded a festively decorated train bound for Texas. A band played, Civil War veterans bid them Godspeed, and wives and sweethearts dabbed their eyes as the train left the station. Pauline O'Neill did not cry, but her "heart was wrung in agony."

The train went first to Flagstaff, then on to Albuquerque and El Paso. When the men finally arrived in San Antonio, they met up with new recruits from Oklahoma and the New Mexico Territory, along with men from the East Coast, the plains of the Midwest, and far reaches of the Northwest. They were issued Krag-Jorgensen rifles and brass-filled cartridge belts. Fresh horses arrived from St. Louis, and the men chose their steeds. Before long the volunteers numbered close to 800; Captain O'Neill's Troop A consisted of three officers and 68 men. After their training as cavalry troops was deemed satisfactory, they were taken by train to Tampa, Florida, where they boarded steamers headed for Cuba. Unfortunately their horses and nearly half the regiment were left behind in Tampa.

Many of the men were seasick during the crowded, 5-1/2-day rocky ride to Cuba. Most had body lice and the food and water was bad. On June 20, when they arrived in Santiago harbor, the seas were rough and the men had to try to jump on a small pier as the boats rose and fell against it. Two Black regulars were thrown into the water when their boat capsized, and Captain O'Neill dove in to try to save them. He could not rescue the men, however, who were dragged under by their heavy equipment. If Spanish troops had been there they could have wiped out the entire landing force.

The heat and humidity of Cuba quickly made life difficult for the men from Arizona. Malaria and other diseases waited for them, and mosquitoes attacked day and night. The Cuban people who greeted them were friendly but desperate, hungry and poor. They had suffered terribly at the hands of the Spanish. The American troops gave away much of what they had, then began making their way through the jungle-like terrain, not knowing quite what to expect. Within a few days they encountered 1,500 Spanish soldiers who fired German Mausers at them. Fifteen American troops including eight Rough Riders were killed. McClintock was shot in the leg and Brodie in the arm. That left Col. Theodore Roosevelt and Capt. Buckey O'Neill in charge.

On July 1, 1898, after days of pouring rain, bad food and small side skirmishes, the Rough Riders were ready to participate in the famous assault on San Juan Heights. First, however, they had to secure a small hill the troops named Kettle Hill because of its sugar refinery and large kettles. Rifle fire rang out from the refinery where the Spanish were entrenched but the distance was too far for the Americans to shoot back effectively. The Spanish were also well hidden and using smokeless powder.

The American troops hunkered down as bullets whistled past. Captain Buckey O'Neill, while trying to keep up the morale of his men, refused to lie low as he paced back and forth with little regard for his own safety. It was said that he had stated several times, "The Spanish bullet is not molded that will kill me." Fate was not kind to Captain O'Neill, however, as it was there, at the base of Kettle Hill, that Buckey's luck ran out and he took a deadly bullet to the head. His men rallied around him and pulled his body out of harm's way, but the hero of Prescott quickly breathed his last. The soldiers had no choice but to bury him in a shallow grave and keep on fighting. After a Gatling gun detachment arrived and was put into operation, the U.S. troops took Kettle Hill and Roosevelt led the charge that captured San Juan Hill. Within weeks the war was over and the Spanish were defeated. An armistice was signed on August 12, 1898.

Pauline O'Neill was devastated upon hearing of her husband's death. The residents of Prescott went into mourning, and people around the territory shook their heads in sadness and disbelief. In the spring of 1899 Buckey's two brothers joined an Army captain and local clergyman in a trip to Cuba where they located Buckey's body and arranged for it to be returned to the United States. On May 1, 1899, ceremonies were held in Arlington National Cemetery outside the nation's Capital as he was laid to rest not far from the grave of his father, Captain John Owen O'Neill, who had fought in the Civil War. Buckey O'Neill never again returned to his home in Prescott. He had lived to be a young man of only 38 years.

When they were on the boat to Cuba, Teddy Roosevelt and Buckey O'Neill had many long talks. Roosevelt later wrote:

Most of the men had simple souls. They could relate facts, and they said very little about what they dimly felt. Buckey O'Neill, however, the iron-nerved, iron-willed fighter from Arizona, the sheriff whose name was a byword of terror to every wrong-doer, white or red, the gambler who with unmoved fact would stake and lose every dollar he had in the world—he, alone with his comrades, was a visionary, an articulate emotionalist. He was very quiet about it, never talking unless he was sure of his listener; but at night when we leaned upon the railing to look up at the Southern Cross, he was less apt to tell tales of his hard and stormy past than he was to speak of the mysteries which lie behind courage, and fear, and love.

George Phippen in 1960 with his canvas
entitled, *Cattle Baron.*
(Louise Phippen)

GEORGE PHIPPEN

The romance of the West and especially of the tall, bronzed cowboy on the trail alongside bawling, dusty cattle have been favorites of Americans since the days of dime novels and black-and-white moving pictures. Many artists have tried to capture this colorful time in history in their work, but few were as successful as self-taught cowboy-artist George Phippen.

Cowboy-artists are not simply western artists; they are true cowboys with first-hand knowledge of working animals, ranch life, and the whims of mother nature. A cowboy-artist is able to infuse his work with the feelings, intensity, and excitement of the life he loves, thereby giving the viewer a true taste of the West—a vision of life on the trail, in the bunkhouse, or out on the prairie. This George Phippen was able to do in grand style.

Born near Charles City, Iowa, in 1915 and raised in Blue Mound, Kansas, George grew up on a farm along with five brothers and three sisters. As a youngster he attended school in a one-room schoolhouse on the Kansas prairie, and his life on the farm consisted of daily chores and working with cattle and horses. As a child he dreamed of the time when he could become a working cowhand and hit the trail like the old-timers who had worked the great cattle drives.

George showed an early talent for drawing, and as a child began sketching animals and modeling them in clay called "Kansas gumbo" that he found in local creek beds. As he gained in age and experience, his clay figures became amazingly life-like. He added cowboys and other animals such as dogs who were animated and full of spirit.

As a young man he talked to the cowboys who had come up the Chisholm Trail on cattle drives. The images that formed in his mind were then transferred to canvas and paper in oil and water color. The anatomy of his human and animal figures was amazingly accurate

213

and life-like. This unusual talent of being able to put down on paper and sculpt in clay the exactness of living creatures would serve George well throughout his lifetime. He was a stickler for detail, and was influenced in his early vision of what western art should be by the paintings of Frederic Remington and Charles Russell. Early on he won numerous prizes for his portrayals of horses and their riders, cattle, and other scenes of life in the West.

In the late 1930s George served in the Civilian Conservation Corps in Minnesota and the state of Washington. It was in Washington that he met Louise, the girl who was to become his wife. They were married in Walla Walla in 1941, and after a short honeymoon George was drafted and joined the Coast Artillery.

When the war ended he and Louise moved to a number of locations where George tried desperately to get started as an artist. They spent five months in Santa Fe, then moved to Phoenix. Finding the heat there unbearable, they towed their 13-foot house trailer to Prescott. When it snowed in October, they drove to Tucson. Finally they came back to Prescott in June 1949. In 1952 George built a log cabin studio in the pines on the outskirts of Prescott. During these years he sold sketches and paintings to galleries, did cartooning and humorous postcard art, and ventured into pen-and-ink illustrations for books and magazines. His work sold well, and as luck would have it, a lucrative new client appeared.

In 1952 a friend introduced him to the president of famed calendar-maker Brown and Bigelow. After being flown to Minnesota where he presented executives with a portfolio of his work, George was given a commission to create western calendar art. In a short time his exciting *Headin' 'Em Off* became a hit. George worked for Brown and Bigelow from 1952-1958. In 1958, after George's contract with Brown and Bigelow expired, the Phippens tried their luck in Grand Junction, Colorado. Then, in 1962, they decided to make their permanent home in Skull Valley, where George set up a studio.

214

As his work began to sell, the Phippens' lifestyle stabilized. Their Skull Valley ranch was a happy place. George and his brother Harold set up the Bear Paw Bronze Works near the studio where they cast George's small bronzes. At that time the art of *lost wax casting* of fine art sculpture was nearly forgotten. George and his brother, along with Joe Noggle and Joe Vest of Prescott, revived the process which lent itself to the growing world of cowboy art. Lynn Phippen, one of George and Louise's sons, remembers witnessing his dad's first crude attempts at casting bronze and the progress he made throughout the years. His brothers Ernie and Loren, who took over the Phippen foundry after George died in 1965, perfected their casting techniques. It was George's pioneering spirit and technical advances, however, along with those of Harold Phippen, Joe Noggle and Joe Vest, that helped produce the phenomenal spread of bronze art—especially western bronze art—for nearly half a century.

George at work on a western painting entitled,
Getting the Mail Through, 1958.
(Louise Phippen)

In addition to painting, sculpting and casting bronze, George and Louise raised four sons and one daughter in the high desert among the cactus and animals they loved. George hand-tooled saddles for his young sons. He brought home assorted animals like burros and even a young mountain lion that was raised by his friend, Whalen Potter. This mountain lion was trained and became a star in Walt Disney movies. Because of Whalen Potter, George acquired animals from Walt Disney Wildlife Productions movie sets in Sedona, including two young black bears featured in Disney's *Yellowstone Cubs* and two full-grown wild Canadian timber wolves featured in *The Legend of Lobo*. These animals were kept behind the Phippen's Skull Valley home in large cages, and the family raised one litter of tame wolf pups. George rapidly became known as a family man and a quiet, sensitive cowboy-artist who produced exquisite work. His paintings and bronzes increased in value

Throughout his life George Phippen mapped out the West with his paints, pens, brushes and clay. He pursued his vision of the cowboy: riding, roping, and tending cattle on the prairie, in the desert, and over the mountains. He finely crafted fiery steeds in clay that were cast in bronze. Human figures such as Father Eusebio Francisco Kino, a Jesuit priest from Italy who traveled throughout the Southwest in the early 1700s, emerged from the raw clay to become the fine bronze that can be seen today in Prescott's Phippen Museum. As the years went by George acquired many friends and patrons of his art, including film star John Wayne, who admired the integrity and exactness of George's work. He even invited the Phippens to San Antonio for a week to watch him film *The Alamo*.

Although George Phippen lived a mere 50 years, he contributed significantly to the world of western art. Called the "master painter for the real west in the mid-20th Century," he was one of the original founders of the Cowboy Artists of America, and its first president. His love of nature, animals and the men and women who helped fashion the West as we know it today are beautifully expressed in the legacy of art works he left behind. It is no wonder, then, that his work continues to be revered and treasured by those who know and appreciate fine western art. Work by George Phippen can be found in many locations across the country, including the National Cowboy Hall of Fame in Oklahoma City; the Phoenix Art Museum; the Gilcrease Institute Museum of Art in Tulsa, Oklahoma; and the Rodeo Hall of Champions and Broadmoor Hotel in Colorado Springs, Colorado. His work can also be seen in an impressive collection in the Desert Caballeros Western Museum in Wickenburg, Arizona (see page 256). Much of Phippen's work is held by private collections. In Prescott, the Phippen Museum is home to several of George's best pieces (see page 109), and his oil painting entitled *The Walker Party in Arizona* is on display in the Prescott Public Library on Goodwin and Marina.

If there's a cowboy heaven, George is sure to be there among his peers, riding and roping with the best of them. In his spare time he is undoubtedly sculpting and painting the working cowboy set against a background of brilliant Arizona sunrises and sunsets that he knew and loved so well. And he is now joined by his beloved wife Louise, who died in January 2001.

George at age 49, working on what would be
one of his last pieces: *Cowboy in a Storm*.
(Louise Phippen)

To be ignorant of what happened
before you were born is to be ever
a child. For what is man's lifetime
unless the memory of past events
is woven with those of earlier times?
(Cicero, *Orator*, Sec. 34)

6. One- and Two-Day Excursions to Areas of Historic Interest

The beautiful city of Prescott sits in the middle of a land of historic riches. If you have an extra day or two to explore the area, consider visiting some of the following attractions:

Camp Verde
Fort Verde State Historic Park

Chino Valley
OK Corral Frontier Museum

Cordes Lakes
Arcosanti

Cottonwood/Clarkdale
Clemenceau Heritage Museum
Verde Canyon Railroad

Flagstaff
Arizona Historical Society Pioneer Museum
Lowell Observatory
Museum of Northern Arizona
Riordan Mansion State Historic Park

Jerome
Gold King Mine and Ghost Town
Jerome State Historic Park (Douglas Mansion)
Mine Museum

Kingman
Army Airfield Historical Society and Museum
Mohave Museum of History and the Arts
Route 66 Museum

Meteor Crater

Payson
Rim Country Museum
Tonto Natural Bridge State Park
Zane Grey Museum

Pioneer Arizona Living History Museum

Sedona
Red Rock State Park
Sedona Heritage Museum

Wickenburg
Desert Caballeros Western Museum
Robson's Arizona Mining World
Vulture Gold Mine

Williams
Grand Canyon Railway
Grand Canyon Railway Museum
Planes of Fame Air Museum

Winslow
La Posada Hotel
Old Trails Museum

In addition to the previously mentioned attractions, northern Arizona offers many National Parks and Monuments that are home to historic buildings, ancient ruins, and Visitor Centers that feature museums and artifacts. Your travels will be much enriched by visiting the following:

Grand Canyon National Park
Bright Angel Lodge
Desert View Watchtower
El Tovar Hotel
Hermits Rest
Hopi House

Montezuma Castle National Monument

Petrified Forest National Park
Painted Desert Inn National Historic Landmark

Sunset Crater Volcano National Monument

Tuzigoot National Monument

Walnut Canyon National Monument

Wupatki National Monument

CAMP VERDE, ARIZONA

Situated just off Interstate 17 directly east of Prescott, this small but interesting town is home to Fort Verde State Historic Park. Founded in 1866, Camp Verde was one of the first military installations in Arizona. The U.S. Army made its presence known during the early days of homesteading, mining, and skirmishes with Apache Native Americans. Visit the **Fort Verde State Historic Park**.

For further information, contact the Camp Verde Chamber of Commerce, 385 South Main Street, P.O. Box 3520, Camp Verde, AZ 86322. Telephone (520)567-9294.

Officers and families, Fort Verde, c. 1890.
(Sharlot Hall Museum, Prescott, Arizona)

FORT VERDE STATE HISTORIC PARK
Box 397, Camp Verde, AZ 86322
(3 miles east of I-17 two blocks off State Road 260)
(520)567-3275

Miles from Prescott: 40

Hours: Daily 8:00 am - 5:00 pm. Closed Christmas Day.

Admission fee: Yes

Established in 1871 and abandoned by the U.S. Army in 1891, Fort Verde today offers several restored buildings, including officers' and surgeon's quarters, that are situated on the old parade ground. Numerous artifacts from days when fort was active are on display in the original administration building.

Restored officers' quarters, Fort Verde.

CHINO VALLEY, ARIZONA

Chino Valley lies approximately 20 miles north of Prescott on State Highway 89, and about 30 miles south of Ash Fork where Highway 89 connects with Interstate 40. Primarily horse and cattle country, Chino Valley is close to the Prescott National Forest and is home to Del Rio Springs, the first military post in northern Arizona that was established in 1863 (Fort Whipple), and the first site of the Arizona Territorial Capital. In 1864 the post and capital were moved to a location just north of downtown Prescott where the Veterans Administration Medical Center is today (see *Histories and Biographies* section under *Fort Whipple* and *Museums* section). Every Labor Day weekend the city holds a big celebration called "First Territorial Capital Days." North of Chino Valley on Highway 89 is the **OK Corral Frontier Museum**. For further information, write to the Chino Valley Chamber of Commerce, P.O. Box 419, Chino Valley AZ 86323. Telephone (520)636-2493. chamber@chinovalley.org; www.chino-valley.org.

OK Corral Frontier Museum
(Ed Klett)

OK CORRAL FRONTIER MUSEUM
6800 State Road 89
P.O. Box 1082
Chino Valley AZ 86323
(520)636-5450

Miles from Prescott: 20

Hours: Daily 9:00 am - 4:00 pm May-September. Winter visits by appointment only.

Admission fee: yes

Five miles north of Chino Valley is a marvelous museum consisting of five buildings full of artifacts situated on 23 acres that is owned and managed by Mr. Ed Klett. A long-time resident of the area, Klett has gathered together a large collection of wagons and buggies from as far back as the Civil War, including U.S. Cavalry wagons and a signal cannon just like the one used by Stonewall Jackson (the cannon balls were heated red-hot before being shot into the enemy camp). Additional displays of old U.S. Army saddles and tack, along with antique furniture and farm equipment, make for a very interesting visit. Families and groups (including school children) are welcome. Please call ahead for a guided tour.

Two Civil War wagons. One on right
is an escort wagon. (Ed Klett)

CORDES LAKES, ARIZONA

Cordes Lakes is a small community situated just east of the junction of Interstate 17 and State Road 69 (exit 262). From the exit **Arcosanti** is two miles down an unpaved road.

Interior of Arcosanti building.

ARCOSANTI
2-1/2 miles east of I-17 and SR 69
HC 74 Box 4136
Mayer, AZ 86333
(520)632-7135   (602)245-5309
www.arcosanti.org

Miles from Prescott: 35

Hours: Daily 9:00 am - 5:00 pm. Closed Thanksgiving and Christmas.

Admission fee: Visitors Center is free; charge for tours.

Community is futuristic; Italian architect and urban planner Paolo Soleri's design combines architecture and ecology to create an atmosphere of concern for humankind and the environment. An ongoing project, Arcosanti is a stunning achievement that draws visitors from all over the world. Workshops are presented regularly, and a music series is scheduled in the summer. Limited lodging is available to visitors for a very modest sum. To support Arcosanti's programs and construction, Soleri's world-famous windbells and other pieces are sold on the premises, at the Cosanti Foundation in Scottsdale, via catalog, and over the internet. Each bell is unique, being made from patina bronze or ceramic, and hallmarked. Cosanti Originals, Inc., is located at 6433 Doubletree Ranch Road, Scottsdale, AZ 85253. Telephone 1-800-752-3187 or (480)948-6145, or go online at www.cosanti.com.

Soleri windbells.

COTTONWOOD/CLARKDALE, ARIZONA

Tucked away in the Verde Valley between Jerome and Sedona lie the thriving communities of Cottonwood and Clarkdale. From here one can also visit Tuzigoot National Monument and Dead Horse Ranch State Park.

Cottonwood was home to soldiers from nearby Fort Verde in the late 1800s, and housed many families whose men worked for the Douglas mining operations in Jerome during the years 1912 through 1953. Visitors to Cottonwood are invited to stroll the streets of Old Town and visit the small but thriving **Clemenceau Heritage Museum**.

Clarkdale housed families of miners who worked for the Clark mining operation in Jerome, and today is the place where travelers can board the **Verde Canyon Railroad.**

For further information, contact the Cottonwood Chamber of Commerce, 1010 South Main Street, Cottonwood, AZ 86326. Telephone (520)634-7593.

CLEMENCEAU HERITAGE MUSEUM
1 North Willard
Cottonwood, AZ 86326

Miles from Prescott: 36

Hours: Wednesday 9:00 am - noon, Friday through Sunday
11:00 am - 3:00 pm. Closed on major holidays.

Admission fee: Donation suggested

Large model railroad display with working trains that depicts the days of
the Verde Valley's large-scale mining and smelting operations. Also a
vintage classroom and other artifacts from the late 1800s and early 1900s
can be seen.

Model railroad display, Clemenceau Heritage Museum.

VERDE CANYON RAILROAD
300 North Broadway
Clarkdale, AZ 86324
(520)639-0010 or (800)293-7245
info@verdecanyonrr.com
www.verdecanyonrr.com

Miles from Prescott: 35

Departures: Call for departure times

Fares: Several classes: First, Coach, over 65, and ages 2-12

A scenic four-hour ride on the Verde Canyon Railroad is available year-round for those wanting the thrill of riding in vintage cars being pulled by two FP7 engines. Passenger cars are climate controlled. Both indoor seating and open-air access available. Narrator onboard. The wilderness excursions take passengers along the Verde River through National Forest land adjacent to the Sycamore Wilderness area near Sedona. Sinagua Indian ruins and varied wildlife can be seen, including bald eagles. Advance reservations required. Small railroad-oriented museum in depot, along with gift shop and cafe.

(Verde Canyon Railroad)

FLAGSTAFF, ARIZONA

Beautiful pine-covered Flagstaff sits at an elevation of nearly 7,000 feet on historic Route 66. One of the important stagecoach stops during the late 1800s, Flagstaff continues to be a major stop on the east-west train routes. Snowy in the winter and cool in the summer, Flagstaff offers much in the way of museums and serves as a gateway to the Grand Canyon and other scenic attractions. Visit the **Arizona Historical Society Pioneer Museum, Lowell Observatory, Museum of Northern Arizona,** and **Riordan Mansion State Historic Park.** Also worth a visit are the Conconino Center for the Arts and Northern Arizona University's Old Main Art Gallery. For further information, contact the Flagstaff Visitor Center, 1 East Route 66, Flagstaff, AZ 86001. Telephone (520)774-9541 or (800)842-7293.

1917 Baldwin steam engine #25 built by Baldwin Locomotive Works in Philadelphia. Used in the early timber and lumber industry, this beauty now sits next to the Flagstaff Visitors' Center.

231

ARIZONA HISTORICAL SOCIETY
PIONEER MUSEUM
2340 North Fort Valley Road
Flagstaff, AZ 86001
(520)774-6272
ahsnad@infomagic.net   www.infomagic.net/^asnad

Miles from Prescott: 90

Hours: Monday through Saturday 9:00 am - 5:00 pm. Closed Sundays, Christmas, New Year's Day, Easter and Thanksgiving

Admission fee: none

The Pioneer Museum has a regular program of changing exhibits in the former Coconino County Hospital (1908) that interpret northern Arizona history. The popular exhibit "Playthings of the Past" can be seen here during the winter holidays. Two major events occur during the summer: (1) the Flagstaff Wool Festival (first weekend in June) that features sheep shearing, spinning, weaving, wool dyeing, camp cooking, and livestock (sheep, goats, alpacas and llamas); and (2) the Independence Day Festival (Fourth of July weekend) that offers living history demonstrations along with woodworking, candle-making, and other crafts. Buildings on the grounds associated with the hospital occupation are the root cellar and 1910 barn. The Ben Doney 1908 homestead cabin was moved here in the 1960s, and a 1929 Baldwin articulated logging locomotive and Sante Fe caboose arrived in 1994. The museum also houses approximately 10,000 area artifacts, a major archival collection of documents, and over 30,000 photographs.

1929 Baldwin articulated locomotive.

LOWELL OBSERVATORY
1400 West Mars Hill Road
Flagstaff, AZ 86001
(520)774-3358
www.lowell.edu

Miles from Prescott: 90

Hours: Daily 9:00 am - 5:00 pm, April-October, with tours at 10, 1 and 3. Daily 12:00 noon - 5:00 pm, November-March, with tours at 1 and 3. Closed Monday and Tuesday in January and February, Thanksgiving, December 24-25, and January 1.

Admission fee: yes

Founded in 1894 by scientist Percival Lowell, the Lowell Observatory is equipped with nine telescopes, including its 24" Clark refracting telescope. It was the discovery site of the planet Pluto in 1930. A video presentation is available to visitors, along with interactive exhibits, guided tours, and nighttime telescope viewing (call for days and times).

The 1916 Slipher Building on Mars Hill where Percival Lowell had his offices and library now houses science staff and administrative offices. The domed Rotunda Library contains historic exhibits.

233

MUSEUM OF NORTHERN ARIZONA
3101 North Fort Valley Road
Flagstaff, AZ 86002
(520)774-5213
www.musnaz.org

Miles from Prescott: 90

Hours: Daily 9:00 am - 5:00 pm. Closed Thanksgiving, Christmas and New Year's Day

Admission fee: yes

Exhibits include geology, anthropology, biology and fine arts of the Colorado Plateau. Hispanic as well as Hopi, Navajo, Pai, and Zuni Native American artists participate in exhibits, sales and special events.

RIORDAN MANSION STATE HISTORIC PARK
409 Riordan Road
Flagstaff, AZ 86001
(520)779-4395
www.pr.state.az.us

Miles from Prescott: 90

Hours: 8:30 am - 5:00 pm daily (May-September), 11:30 am- 5:00 pm (October - April). Closed Christmas. Guided tours on the hour.

Admission fee: yes

Historic 1904, 40-room mansion filled with original furnishings that was built by Flagstaff pioneer lumber barons Timothy and Michael Riordan. An extensive collection of original Stickley furniture can be seen throughout the home. Beautiful wooded setting with picnic benches makes this a very nice place to spend a few hours.

JEROME, ARIZONA

History and amazing sights greet visitors to the copper mining town of Jerome, which thrived as a boom town in the late 1800s and early 1900s. People came from all over the world to work in the mines and run the town, which was essentially shut down after fires plagued the mine tunnels and numerous other factors such as labor unrest made them unprofitable. Today buildings teeter on steep slopes and old homes and businesses look a lot like they did in Jerome's heyday when 15,000 people lived there.

Located on State Road 89A north of Prescott, a good 1-1/2-hour drive up a steep, winding road, Jerome offers visitors a trip back into time when copper reigned supreme. Jerome was declared a National Historic Landmark in 1976. This picturesque town is now home to artists, artisans, musicians, historians, business owners and their families. Everyone is welcome year 'round to visit the museums, shops and galleries, and to explore the town. Visit the **Gold King Mine and Ghost Town, Jerome State Historic Park (Douglas Mansion)**, and **Mine Museum.**

For further information contact the Jerome Chamber of Commerce, 317 Hullave, P.O. Box K, Jerome, AZ 86331. Telephone (520)634-2900. www.jeromechamber.com.

GOLD KING MINE AND GHOST TOWN
P.O. Box 125
Jerome, AZ 86331
(520)634-0053
www.goldkingmineghosttown1.bizonthe.net

Miles from Prescott: 35

Hours: 9:00 am - 5:00 pm daily. Closed Thanksgiving and Christmas.

Admission fee: yes

Located one mile south of Jerome, the Gold King Mine was once Haynes, Arizona, home of the Haynes Copper Company. Today the town offers historic buildings, mine visits, and demonstrations of antique mining equipment and vehicles.

JEROME STATE HISTORIC PARK
(DOUGLAS MANSION)
Box D
Jerome, AZ 86331
(520)634-5381

Miles from Prescott: 34

Hours: 8:00 am - 5:00 pm daily. Closed Christmas.

Admission fee Yes

Historic mansion and grounds formerly owned by the Douglas family, this elegant home was built in 1916 by "Rawhide Jimmy" Douglas. It is located next to the Little Daisy Mine. Exhibits include artifacts, photos, mining equipment, and an excellent video presentation.

MINE MUSEUM
200 Main Street
Jerome, AZ 86331
(520)634-5477

Miles from Prescott: 34

Museum Hours: 9:00 am - 4:30 pm daily. Gift shop open 9:00 am - 5:00 pm daily. Closed Thanksgiving and Christmas.

Admission fee: yes

Artifacts, photos and paintings telling of Jerome's unusual and colorful history are displayed in this unique museum.

KINGMAN, ARIZONA

Founded as a railroad town in 1882 and located on historic Route 66, Kingman sits at a major crossroads of I-40 and State Road 93 that takes travelers headed north across the Hoover Dam and on to Las Vegas. From Kingman one can also explore historic Chloride, Oatman and Peach Springs. Kingman hosts many events that draw numerous visitors including the Historic Route 66 Road Rally, the Andy Devine Days PRCA Rodeo, and the Mohave County Fair. Visit the **Army Airfield Museum** (opening in early 2001), **Bonelli House, Mohave Museum of History and Arts** and the **Route 66 Museum** (opening May 2001). Across Route 66 from the Visitors Center (located in the recently restored Powerhouse building) in **Locomotive Park** is famed steam locomotive #3759, the last steam engine used by the Santa Fe Railroad to pull into Kingman. It is accompanied by a vintage caboose.

For further information contact the Kingman Chamber of Commerce, 120 W. Andy Devine Avenue, P.O. Box 1150, Kingman, AZ 86402-1150. Telephone (602)753-6253.

Locomotive #3759.

ARMY AIRFIELD HISTORICAL SOCIETY
AND MUSEUM
4540 Flightline Drive
Kingman, AZ 86401
(520)757-1892 (days)   (520)753-6036 (evenings)

Miles from Prescott: 142

Hours: 10:00 am - 3:00 pm Monday-Friday, weekends by appointment.
Call Kingman Chamber of Commerce for further information.

Admission fee: donation requested

Once home to 7,000 Army Air Forces bombers, fighters and training
planes left in the desert after World War II, the five-square-mile former
gunnery base and storage depot was slowly phased out by the military in
the 1950s and the planes sold as salvage. A museum highlighting the
airfield's years of glory when 48,000 men trained here is now open in one
of the four remaining original hangars. Large group tours available by
appointment.

B-17s after World War II.
(Courtesy of the Mohave Museum of History & Arts #7910)

MOHAVE MUSEUM OF HISTORY AND ARTS
400 West Beale Street
Kingman, AZ 86401
(520)753-3195
mocohist@ctaz.com
www.ctaz.com/~mocohist/museum/index.htm

Miles from Prescott: 142

Hours: 9:00 am - 5:00 pm Monday-Friday, 1:00 pm - 5:00 pm Saturday and Sunday. Closed major holidays.

Admission fee: yes

Photos and artifacts depicting the history of the area, along with displays portraying the life of Mohave and Hualapai Native American people are spaciously exhibited. Special display on hometown movie star Andy Devine. Copies of Lawrence Williams' portraits of United States Presidents and their wives (originals in Smithsonian) grace the walls. Outdoor exhibits include wagons, mining equipment, farm machinery, and a 19th-century Santa Fe caboose. Museum is located across from Locomotive Park.

ROUTE 66 MUSEUM
120 West Andy Devine Avenue
(Historic Powerhouse Building)
Kingman, AZ 86402
(Opening May 2001)

Miles from Prescott: 142

Hours: Daily 9:00 am - 5:00 pm December-February; 9:00 am - 6:00 pm March-November. Closed Christmas, New Year's, Easter and Thanksgiving.

Admission fee: yes

At long last there will be a museum that will officially honor the great Mother Road in Arizona and the people who traveled her. The new Route 66 Museum, located in the 1904 Desert Power and Light Building near the Visitor Center, is the result of many dedicated Kingman residents who strove for years to create a tribute not only to Route 66, but to the 35th Parallel and its many roads and trails. First there were native trading trails, then the Beale wagon road, the Santa Fe Railroad and, for 50 years, Route 66.

Exhibits will include a prairie schooner replica and the story of a typical family that traversed northern Arizona in one of these wondrous crafts. Depression-era artifacts will be on display, including old photos and a 1929 pickup truck. The 1950s will be represented by a classic Studebaker and a street-front scene depicting a small town main street. Housed in the museum will also be an archival deposit of information about Route 66 that will be maintained by the Historic Route 66 Association of Arizona.

1950 Studebaker

243

Route 66 Museum.

Conestoga replica.

METEOR CRATER
Just off Interstate 40 between Flagstaff and Winslow
P.O. Box 70
Flagstaff, AZ 86002-0070
(520)289-5898
Crater: (520)289-2362 * RV Park: (520)289-4002
www.meteorcrater.com
www.info@meteorcrater.com

Miles from Prescott: 125

Hours: 6:00 am - 6:00 pm daily May 15-September 15, 8:00 am - 5:00 pm daily September 16 - May 14. Open 365 days of the year.

Admission fee: yes

The 570-foot-deep, one-mile-wide Meteor Crater is the best- preserved meteorite impact site on earth. It is a designated Natural Landmark by the Department of the Interior, and is a training site for Apollo astronauts. Exhibits and video presentations in the Museum discuss Astrogeology. Numerous meteorites are presented. Original Apollo Space Capsule is on display.

(Meteor Crater, Northern Arizona, USA)

245

PAYSON

Scenic Payson is located 5,000 feet high in the ponderosa pines on th edge of the Mogollon Rim. It is home to the annual World's Oldest Continuous Rodeo, and hosts a old time fiddlers' contest, blues festival, and equestrian events each year. In recent years Payson has emerged as a fine arts center and is home to famous artists. Within the town limits reside the Tonto Apache Reservation and the Mazatzal Casino. Payson is also home to the **Rim Country Museum** and the **Zane Grey Museum**. Nearby are the Shoofly Village archeological site, **Tonto Natural Bridge State Park,** and the Tonto Fish Hatchery. The rim country is famous for its wild life, lakes and fishing streams, and Payson and the surrounding area offer approximately 600 motel/hotel rooms. For further information contact the Rim Country Regional Chamber of Commerce, 100 West Main Street, P.O. Box 1380, Payson, AZ 85547. Telephone (520)474-4515 or (800)672-9766. Fax (520)474-8812. rcrc@rimcountrychamber.com   www.rimcountrychamber.com.

PINE and STRAWBERRY

Just north of Payson on State Road 87 are the small communities of Pine and Strawberry that boast a very interesting museum as well as the Strawberry Schoolhouse, the oldest standing schoolhouse in Arizona. Pine was settled in 1879 by Mormon pioneers. The community hosts a yearly Strawberry Festival. For further information contact the Rim Country Regional Chamber of Commerce at the address given above.

RIM COUNTRY MUSEUM
700 Green Valley Parkway
P.O. Box 2532
Payson, AZ 85547
(520)474-3483
searchers@netzone.com   members.nbci.com/rimmuseum

Miles from Prescott: 90

Hours: 12:00 pm - 4:00 pm Wednesday-Sunday. Closed major holidays.

Admission fee: yes

Historic buildings including 1930 forest ranger's residence, replica of old Herron Hotel, and 1907 forest ranger's station are on the grounds. Original fire-fighting equipment is on display. Exhibits depict and explain story of ancient peoples who lived in the area from 300-1300 A.D. Future plans are to build a cabin similar to that used by writer Zane Grey when he wrote several of his books that have a Mogollon Rim location.

TONTO NATURAL BRIDGE STATE PARK
P.O. Box 1245
Payson, AZ 85547-1245
(520)476-4202

Miles from Prescott: 85

Hours: 8:00 am - 7:00 pm daily May-September, 9:00 am- 5:00 pm daily October-April. Closed Christmas.

Admission fee: yes

Tonto Natural Bridge is thousands of years old and is believed to be the largest natural travertine bridge in the world. A true geologic wonder, Tonto Natural Bridge is an incredible sight to behold. The historic lodge housed within the park has been restored and contains period furnishings. Picnic tables, restrooms and gift shop on site.

ZANE GREY MUSEUM
503 West Main Street, Suite B
Payson, AZ 85541
(520)474-6243 fax (520)474-3294
zgm@pobox.com

Miles from Prescott: 90

Hours: 10:00 am - 3:00 pm Monday-Saturday; 12:00 noon - 4:00 pm Sunday. Closed major holidays.

Admission: yes

Housed in a small building on Main Street, the manager and curator of the Zane Grey Museum have set up a fine display that includes memorabilia such as letters, photos, guns and fishing rods, and a complete set of author Grey's novels. A video presentation is also available. Grey came to Arizona in 1918 and wrote 36 of his famous novels in and around Payson, including *The Last of the Plainsmen* and *Man of the Forest*. His last visit to Payson was in 1929.

PIONEER ARIZONA
LIVING HISTORY MUSEUM

The Pioneer Arizona Living History Museum is located just off Interstate 17 several miles north of Phoenix at Exit 225, within easy driving distance from Prescott. It is well worth the trip or a stop if you are driving between the two cities. It is the largest living history museum west of the Rockies.

Old opera house.

PIONEER ARIZONA LIVING HISTORY MUSEUM
3901 West Pioneer Road
Phoenix, AZ 85027
(I-17, one mile north of Carefree Highway)
(623)465-1052   fax (623)465-0683

Miles from Prescott: 60

Hours: 9:00 am - 5:00 pm Wednesday-Sunday, year-round. Closed Monday and Tuesday.

Admission fee: yes

Twenty-eight historic buildings, including an opera house, church, ranch complex, sheriff's office, blacksmith shop and schoolhouse are situated on 90 acres. Live interpreters and re-enactors can usually be found on the grounds of this marvelous museum to help explain life as it was lived long ago. Full-service restaurant open 8:00 am - 2:30 pm. Gift shop. Horseback riding and wagon rides available. Weddings in church. Field trips for students and groups.

Victorian house.

SEDONA, ARIZONA

There are not enough words in the English language to describe the stunning beauty of Sedona and its environs. The brilliant red rock vistas that greet visitors coming into town on either State Road 89A or 179 never lessen in their impact. Visitors from the United States and the rest of the world come to Sedona year-round to take photographs, hike, shop, and enjoy the beautiful scenery. Tucked away on Jordan Road just behind the uptown area is an old West museum run by the Sedona Historical Society, the **Sedona Heritage Museum**. A little over five miles south of Sedona's "Y" (intersection of Highways 89A and 179) and three miles east on Lower Red Rock Loop Road is the lovely **Red Rock State Park**. Be sure to visit both. For further information write to the Sedona-Oak Creek Canyon Chamber of Commerce, P.O. Box 478, Sedona AZ 86339. Telephone (800)288-7336 or (520)282-7722. www.VisitSedona.com.

RED ROCK STATE PARK
4050 Red Rock Loop Road
Sedona, AZ 86336
(520)282-6907   fax (520)282-5972
jschreiber@pr.state.az.us   www.pr.state.az.us

Miles from Prescott: 55 (via steep, winding State Road 89A through Jerome and Cottonwood), or 95 via State Roads 69 and 169 and I-17).

Hours: 8:00 am - 6:00 pm daily April-September; 8:00 - 5:00 pm daily October-March. Closed Christmas Day. Visitor Center open daily 9:00 am - 5:00 pm all year.

Admission fee: yes

If you visit Sedona and want to get away from the busy city-center, take a drive to Red Rock State Park. Here it's quiet and beautiful, and the park's six-mile trail network beckons those who want to view nature at its best. None of the trails are extremely strenuous, and one is suitable for wheelchairs. The park has a visitor center that offers nature and bird walks, hikes, assorted exhibits, and video presentations. It also has "hands-on" experiences for children and a gift shop. Picnic areas with grills are available. Weddings by arrangement.

SEDONA HERITAGE MUSEUM
(AND APPLE BARN)
in Jordan Historical Park
735 Jordan Road, P.O. Box 10216
Sedona, AZ 86339
(520)282-7038
info@Sedonamuseum.org   www.sedonamuseum.org

Miles from Prescott: 61 (via steep, winding State Road 89A through Jerome and Cottonwood) or 90 (via State Roads 69 and 169 and I-17).

Hours: Daily 11:00 am - 4:00 pm. Last tour at 3:00 pm. Closed major holidays.

Admission fee: yes

This restored 1930s ranch house is filled with authentic furnishings and artifacts, including an exhibit on films made in the Sedona area. Vintage buggies, tractors and fire-fighting equipment, and a 40-foot-long apple-processing machine are also on display. Special tour arrangements by appointment.

WICKENBURG, ARIZONA

In 1863 Henry Wickenburg's discovery of gold approximately 20 miles southwest of the city of Wickenburg set off an enormous gold rush that brought in prospectors from across the country. The mine that made the area famous was the Vulture Gold Mine. By 1966 Wickenburg had become the third largest city in Arizona. Today the area is known for its many ranches, especially guest ranches. Other notable attractions are the **Desert Caballeros Western Museum, Robson's Arizona Mining World,** and the historic **Vulture Gold Mine.** Other things to see are the old #761 Santa Fe steam locomotive behind the Municipal Center.

For further information, contact the Wickenburg Chamber of Commerce, which is housed in the historic Santa Fe Depot, 216 North Frontier Street, Wickenburg, Arizona 85358. Telephone (520)684-5479 or (800)942-5242. www.wickenburgchamber.com.

Thanks for the Rain by Joe Beeler, C.A.A.

NOTE: *To avoid the steepest part of State Road 89 south from Prescott to Wickenburg, take Iron Springs Road west out of Prescott through Skull Valley to Kirkland, then head east to Kirkland Junction which will connect with SR 89.*

DESERT CABALLEROS WESTERN MUSEUM
21 North Frontier Street
Wickenburg, AZ 85390
(520)684-2272   fax (520)684-5794
info@westernmuseum.org   www.westernmuseum.org

Miles from Prescott: 60 via steep, winding State Road 89 (see Note on page 255).

Hours: 10:00 am - 5:00 pm Monday-Saturday, 12:00 pm - 4:00 pm Sunday. Closed New Year's Day, Easter, July 4, Thanksgiving and Christmas.

Admission fee: yes

Paintings, sculptures and drawings by noted western artists, including Frederic Remington and Charles Russell, can be seen in this outstanding museum. Native American art and artifacts are also on display, along with desert frontier period rooms of 100 years ago, early working cowboy gear, minerals and gems. This museum ties together art of the cowboy such as ornate tooling on spurs with art featuring the cowboy and rural Arizona history, especially during the late frontier period. Pieces by members of the Cowboy Artists of America and the Taos Society of Artists are featured. In the museum park is an outstanding bronze entitled *Thanks for the Rain* by Joe Beeler, C.A.A. Special exhibits and educational programs take place throughout the year.

ROBSON'S ARIZONA MINING WORLD
P.O. Box 3465
(State Road 71 between mileposts 89 & 90)
Wickenburg, AZ 85358
(520)685-2609
www.azoutback.com

Miles from Prescott: 65 via steep, winding State Road 89 to State Road 71; 21 miles south on 71 (see Note on page 255). Watch for figure of Indian astride horse.

Hours: 10:00 am - 4:00 pm Monday-Friday and 8:00 am - 6:00 pm Saturday and Sunday, October 1 - May 1. Closed May 2 - September 31.

Admission fee: yes

Antique mining equipment and 30 artifact-filled buildings make up the major displays on the grounds of this amazing museum. Native American artifacts and petroglyphs can be viewed. Hiking trails are available, and gold can be panned for a fee. Bed and breakfast available at Litsch's Boarding House. Full-service restaurant and ice cream parlor on the premises. Most of grounds is wheelchair-accessible.

VULTURE GOLD MINE
Contact: John and Marge Osborne
36610 North 355ᵗʰ Avenue
Wickenburg, AZ 85390
(602)859-2743
www.jpc-training.com/vulture.htm

Miles from Prescott: 75 via steep, winding State Road 89 to State Road 93. South to 93/60 junction, then east on 60 2-1/2 miles to Vulture Mine Road (see Note on page 255).

Hours: Daily 8:00 am - 4:00 pm during the winter. For summer hours call the Wickenburg Chamber of Commerce (602)684-5479.

Admission fee: yes

Many original buildings, unrestored, can be visited at this fascinating mine site, including the 1884 assay office, stamp mill, and blacksmith shop. Henry Wickenburg's original house is still there, along with the famous "hanging tree" where 18 "high-graders" or gold thieves were strung up during the late 1800s. Above-ground self-guided walking tours available with paid admission. Underground walking mine tours available in groups of six or more by appointment only. It's been said that 2-3 times the amount of gold taken out is still in the ground. Mine is currently for sale.

WILLIAMS

Historic Route 66 goes right through the heart of the quaint railroad town of Williams, Arizona. Here visitors can catch a glimpse of days of yore when Williams was a major logging center. Located in the pines just off Interstate 40 at exit 153, it is situated at the base of State Road 64, which leads to the south rim of the Grand Canyon. The historic Fray Marcos Hotel is the place to stay before catching a train on the **Grand Canyon Railway**, and the well-preserved **Williams Depot** offers a small but charming museum that contains numerous exhibits. Here also is information about the Harvey Girls and the Harvey chain of restaurants and hotels that were so popular when trains were the main means of travel from east to west. Golf, hiking, mountain biking and fishing are popular pastimes in Williams year-round, and the Williams ski area offers winter sports. Old town offers arts, crafts, and antique shops.

For further information, contact the Williams-Grand Canyon/U.S. Forest Service Visitor Center, 200 West Railroad Avenue, Williams, Arizona 86046. Telephone (520)635-4061. The Williams Chamber of Commerce can be reached at 635-1418 during regular business hours.

GRAND CANYON RAILWAY
(Departs from Williams, Arizona)
1201 West Route 66, Suite 200
Flagstaff, AZ 86001
1-800-843-8724
www.thetrain.com

Miles from Prescott: 64

Departure: 10:00 am daily
Does not run December 24 and 25

Return: 5:45 pm (3-1.2 hours in Grand Canyon National
Park; bus tours offered in park)

Fares: Several classes: Coach, Club, First, Deluxe
Observation and Luxury Parlor Car

If you'd like to arrive at the south rim of the Grand Canyon in grand style, consider taking the Grand Canyon Railway from Williams. You will ride in vintage coaches being pulled by a turn-of-the-century steam locomotive in summer and a 1950s diesel in winter. Be serenaded by western entertainers and watch for wildlife along the way. Grand Canyon Railway connects with Amtrak and offers hotel packages at the Fray Marcos Hotel.

(Grand Canyon Railway)

GRAND CANYON RAILWAY MUSEUM
Williams Depot
233 North Grand Canyon Boulevard
Williams, AZ 86046

Miles from Prescott: 64

Hours: 9:00 am - 5:30 pm daily. Closed December 24-25.

Admission fee: no

Railroad artifacts and displays are the main focus of this small but interesting museum housed in the 1908 Williams Depot. Mining, ranching and logging exhibits and photos can also be seen, along with information on the Fred Harvey Railway hotels that reigned supreme during the golden years of train travel in the West.

PLANES OF FAME AIR MUSEUM
State Road 64 and Federal Highway 180
HCR 34, Box B
Valle-Williams, AZ 86046
(520)635-1000
www.planesoffame.org

Miles from Prescott: 92

Hours: daily 9:00 am - 6:00 pm summer; 9:00 am - 5:00 pm winter. Closed Christmas and Thanksgiving.

Admission fee: yes

Thirty vintage aircraft, several of which are flyable, can be seen in this unique museum approximately 28 miles north of Williams. Among the aircraft on display are General Douglas MacArthur's personal Lockheed C-121A Constellation; North American F-86-A Sabre; North American P-51A Mustang; Messerschmidt Bf109-G-10; and Grumman F-11F1 Tiger. Other exhibits include numerous artifacts and memorabilia, plus a Women in Aviation exhibit. A new attraction is a 5x12-foot wind tunnel built by aerospace engineering students at Embry-Riddle Aeronautical University in Prescott.

RB-26C Invader.
(Planes of Fame Air Museum)

WINSLOW

Once a booming railroad town, historic Winslow now sits quietly but not unnoticed on the famous Route 66 just off Interstate 40, 58 miles east of Flagstaff and 148 miles from Prescott. In the early days of travel by wagon, Winslow was on the Beale Trail and Mormon Honeymoon Trail. Later it was a stagecoach stop on the main line between Albuquerque and Prescott. When the Santa Fe Railway hit its peak passenger traffic in the 1920s, folks from the East flocked to places like the Painted Desert and Grand Canyon, stopping in Winslow along the way. Today trains still roll through town every few minutes, and history and nostalgia buffs drive Route 66, looking for vestiges of the time when the great mother road brought cars across the country from Chicago to Los Angeles.

Several things make Winslow a great overnight destination, including the fact that it is home to the last great railroad hotel designed and decorated in 1930 by Mary Jane Colter (see *Histories and Biographies* section): **La Posada**. In addition, Winslow houses the **Old Trails Museum** and is centrally located for exploring important natural wonders like the Petrified Forest and Painted Desert. For more information write to the Winslow Chamber of Commerce, P.O. Box 460, Winslow, AZ 86047. Telephone (602)289-2434.

LA POSADA HOTEL
303 East Second Street
Winslow, AZ 86047
(520)289-4366   fax (520)289-3873
laposadahotel@earthlink.net
www.laposada.org

Miles from Prescott: 148

Hours: Open daily 8:00 am - 8:00 pm for self-guided tours. Guided tours by appointment only.

Admission fee: Donation requested

Photos and artifacts from the days when La Posada was in full operation as the last of the great Fred Harvey Railway hotels can be seen throughout this marvelous structure. Featured is information on Mary Jane Colter and how she designed the hotel and its gardens. Also on display are original furnishings designed by Colter, and memorabilia from the days of the Harvey Girls.

This beautiful hotel built in 1930 is being authentically restored room by room based on original photos and written descriptions. Guest rooms are furnished with antiques and historic photos. Room rates are modest, and the train still stops only a few steps from the front entrance. La Posada also offers the Turquoise Restaurant and a gift shop where one can buy dinnerware designed by Mary Jane Colter. A National Historic Landmark, La Posada should not be missed.

Front of La Posada Hotel.

Interior designed by Mary Jane Colter.

OLD TRAILS MUSEUM
212 Kinsley Avenue
Winslow AZ 86047
(520)289-5861
oldtrails@cybertails.com

Miles from Prescott: 148

Hours: 1:00 pm -5:00 pm Tuesday-Saturday. Closed major holidays.

Admission fee: no

Photos and artifacts relating to historic Route 66, the Beale and Mormon Honeymoon Trails. Other exhibits include Santa Fe Railroad and Fred Harvey memorabilia, along with artifacts related to ranch life, territorial medicine, and small town life in northern Arizona. Be sure to visit this small but very interesting museum when you are in Winslow.

NATIONAL PARKS AND MONUMENTS

Northern Arizona is home to many extraordinary United States National Parks and Monuments. The Grand Canyon requires at least one full day for visitors to see and appreciate but a portion of its breathtaking grandeur. The other parks and monuments mentioned below can be viewed in half a day, but more time is needed for hiking or leisurely exploration. Each has an excellent visitor center staffed by knowledgeable park rangers, and contains important artifacts and exhibits relevant to the park and its surrounding area. Included in this section are the following:

- Grand Canyon National Park
- Montezuma Castle National Monument
- Petrified Forest National Park
- Sunset Crater Volcano National Monument
- Tuzigoot National Monument
- Walnut Canyon National Monument
- Wupatki National Monument

For a full listing of National Park Service sites in Arizona, log on to www.nps.gov.

GRAND CANYON NATIONAL PARK
P.O. Box 129
Grand Canyon, AZ 86023-0129
(520)638-7888 (recorded)
www.grand-canyon.com
www.kaibab.org
www.thecanyon.com

Lodging:
Grand Canyon National Park Lodges
P.O. Box 699
Grand Canyon, AZ 86023
(800)221-2222 (303)297-2757
Camping: (800)365-2267

Miles from Prescott: 120

Admission fee: yes

The Grand Canyon, one of nature's most spectacular creations, can be reached easily in one day from Prescott. The drive is most direct by taking State Road 89 north to Interstate 40, drive east to Williams, then north on State Road 64 which joins with 180. This route will take you first to Tusayan, where numerous places of lodging can be found, and finally to the entrance of the South Rim of the canyon. There is also a train run by the Grand Canyon Railway that departs daily from Williams to the South Rim (see page 260).

Within the park on the South Rim are several historic buildings that offer accommodations and have been mentioned previously in the *Histories and Biographies* section under the heading *Mary Jane Colter*. Within their walls can be found beautiful paintings and decor, and historic artifacts. These include the El Tovar Hotel (1905), Bright Angel Lodge (1935), and Phantom Ranch (at the bottom—reached by mule ride down face of canyon) (1922). Also on the South Rim are Colter's creations Hopi House (1905), Hermits Rest and Lookout Studio (1914); and the Watchtower (1932).

The South Rim is open year-round, but Hermits Rest Drive is closed to private vehicles from March 1 - November 30. Hiking trails abound; horseback riding is available. Mule rides to the bottom with an overnight stay at Phantom Ranch require an advance reservation. Call (303)297-2757.

Mary Jane Colter's Watchtower.

Historic Hopi House.

Mary Jane Colter's fireplace in Bright Angel Lodge.

MONTEZUMA CASTLE
NATIONAL MONUMENT
P.O. Box 219
Camp Verde, AZ 86322
(520)567-3322
www.nps.gov/moca

Miles from Prescott: 41

Admission fee: yes

Hours: 8:00 am - 7:00 pm Memorial Day-Labor Day; 8:00 am - 5:00 pm rest of year.

Visitors to **Montezuma Castle** will be astounded by this five-story structure containing 20 rooms that is nestled in the recess of a large cliff. It was initially begun by Sinagua farmers in the 12th Century as a dwelling place that offered security, fertile land, and nearby water. The visitor's center presents artifacts and exhibits telling of the Sinagua people. Its location is just off I-17 at Exit 289. Nearby is **Montezuma Well**, which is a limestone sink where both Sinagua and Hohokam people lived and farmed.

PETRIFIED FOREST NATIONAL PARK
P.O. Box 2217,
Petrified Forest, AZ 86028-2217
(520)524-6228
www.nps.gov/pefo

Miles from Prescott: 202

Admission fee: yes

Hours: 8:00 am - 5:00 pm daily. Closed Christmas.

Although this wondrous part of the National Park system in Arizona is quite some distance from Prescott, it is well worth the time and effort if you want to see a very beautiful and unique place that was once the home of ancient reptiles, amphibians, and small dinosaurs. The Petrified Forest is strewn with the remains of 225-million-year-old trees that have turned to colorful stone. They can be seen on a 28-mile drive that begins off State Road 180 or Exit 311 off I-40. A 20-minute park film is shown in the Painted Desert Visitor Center where local area information is on display. The Painted Desert itself is a panorama of multicolored rock strata that is most evident in the northern part of the park. Visit the Painted Desert Inn, which has been designated a National Historic Landmark. This famous structure was one of Mary Jane Colter's decorating projects in 1947 (see *Histories and Biographies* section under *Mary Jane Colter*). Fred Kabotie murals are preserved on interior walls. Humans lived in the area for more than 10,000 years, and displays of early habitation can be seen in the Painted Desert Inn, Puerco Pueblo, Newspaper Rock, and Agate House.

Fred Kabotie mural.

Fallen tree (Agate Bridge) in Petrified Forest.

Painted Desert Inn.

SUNSET CRATER VOLCANO
NATIONAL MONUMENT
6400 North Highway 89
Flagstaff, AZ 86004
(520)526-0502

Miles from Prescott: 102

Admission fee: yes

Hours: Daily 9:00 am - 5:00 pm December-February; 8:00 am - 5:00 pm March-May and September-November; 8:00 am - 6:00 pm June-August. Closed Christmas. May also close in winter due to snow.

When one thinks of Arizona, hot dry deserts come to mind. Just north of Flagstaff, however, surrounded by lush green forests, is a mighty volcano surrounded by lava fields that will astound you. Sunset Crater Volcano is a 1000-foot cinder cone made up of varied color cinder that exhibits a rosy crest at sunset. It first erupted nearly 1,000 years ago but the lava flow looks as if it happened only yesterday. A self-guided trail is available to visitors and picnic facilities are available.

TUZIGOOT NATIONAL MONUMENT
P.O. Box 219
Camp Verde, AZ 86322
(520)567-3322
www.nps.gov/tuzi

Miles from Prescott: 38

Admission fee: yes

Hours: Daily 8:00 am - 7:00 pm Memorial Day-Labor Day; 8:00 am - 5:00 pm rest of year. Closed Christmas.

Tuzigoot is an amazing Sinaguan pueblo built between 1125 and 1400 that has survived in relatively good condition. It is part of a large village that was originally two stories high and had 77 ground-floor rooms. As with the Montezuma Castle visitor center, Tuzigoot offers exhibits and artifacts that tell of the lives of the Sinaguan people who inhabited this land so long ago. Tuzigoot is located just outside Clarkdale and Cottonwood off State Road 89A. Exit I-17 at State Road 260 and head north.

WALNUT CANYON NATIONAL MONUMENT
Walnut Canyon Road
Flagstaff, AZ 86004-9705
(520)526-3367
www.nps.gov/waca

Miles from Prescott: 102

Admission fee: yes

Hours: Daily 9:00 am - 5:00 pm December-February; 8:00 am - 5:00 pm March-May; 8:00 am - 6:00 pm June-August; 8:00 am - 5:00 pm September-November. Closed Christmas.

Walnut Canyon harbors hundreds of cliff dwellings once inhabited by the Sinagua people, ancestors of the Hopi, who left the Flagstaff area around 1250. They farmed the top of the canyon and lived in the shelter of the rock face caves. The visitor center exhibits artifacts from the settlement. Foot trails begin outside the door to view the cliff dwellings; one descends 185 feet. Picnic area available. Walnut Canyon is just east of Flagstaff off I-40 at exit 204.

(National Park Service)

WUPATKI NATIONAL MONUMENT
HC33, Box 444A
Flagstaff, AZ 86004
(520)679-2365
www.nps.gov/wupa

Miles from Prescott: 130

Admission fee: yes

Hours: Daily 9:00 am - 5:00 pm all year, with extended hours in the summer. Closed Christmas.

The vast Wupatki National Monument with its five major pueblos is situated in the quiet land just north of Flagstaff (approximately 20 miles north of Flagstaff off State Road 89). A loop road connects Wupatki with Sunset Crater Volcano National Monument. About 800 years ago this area was farmed by an extended indigenous community that left numerous housing structures for us to view. The visitor center offers many exhibits telling about this outstanding part of northern Arizona. Many trails allow visitors access to the pueblos.

The use of travelling is to regulate
imagination by reality, and instead
of thinking how things may be, to
see them as they are.
(Samuel Johnson, Piozzi,
Johnsoniana. No. 154)

Bibliography

BOOKS

Barnett, Franklin, *Viola Jimulla: The Indian Chieftess*, Prescott Yavapai Indians, Prescott, AZ, 1968

Brandes, Ray, *Frontier Military Posts of Arizona*, Dale Stuart King, Publisher, Globe, AZ, 1960

Brown, Margie, *Arizona Pioneers Home Cemetery*, Northern Arizona Genealogy Society, 1994

Brown, Margie, *I.O.O.F. Cemetery*, Northern Arizona Genealogy Society, 1994

Brown, Margie, *Masonic Cemetery*, Northern Arizona Genealogy Society, 1994

Brown, Margie and Grant, *Prescott National Cemetery*, Northern Arizona Genealogy Society, 1995

Brown, Margie, *Rolling Hills Cemetery*, Northern Arizona Genealogy Society, 1993

Brown, Margie, *Simmons Cemetery*, Northern Arizona Genealogy Society, 1993

Davies, A. Mervyn, *Solon H. Borglum, "A Man Who Stands Alone,"* Pequot Press, Chester, CT, 1974

Grattan, Virginia L., *Mary Colter, Builder Upon the Red Earth*, Northland Press, Flagstaff, AZ, 1980

Heckethorn, Ada Fancher, *The Toll Road: Prescott to Fort Mojave*, Pioneer Heritage Publishing, Prescott, AZ, 1997

Herner, Charles, *The Arizona Rough Riders*, The University of Arizona Press, Tucson, AZ, 1970

The Home Book of Quotations, selected and arranged by Burton Stevenson, 10th Ed., Dodd, Mead & Company, New York, 1967

Johnson, Ginger, *Kate T. Kory, Artist of Arizona, 1861-1958*, 1996

Lummis, Charles F., *General Crook and the Apache Wars*, Northland Press, Flagstaff, AZ, 1966

Maxwell, Margaret F., *A Passion for Freedom: The Life of Sharlot Hall*, The University of Arizona Press, Tucson, AZ, 1982

Nelson, Kitty Jo Parker, and Gail A. Gardner, *Prescott's First Century 1864-1964*, reprinted from *Arizoniana: The Journal of Arizona History*, Vol. 4, No. 4, Winter 1963

Ruffner, Melissa, *Prescott: A Pictorial History*, Primrose Press, Prescott, AZ, 1981

Ruland-Thorne, Kate, *The Yavapai: People of the Red Rocks, People of the Sun*, Thorne Enterprises Publications, Inc., Sedona, AZ 1995

Stewart, Tabori & Chang, Inc., *The Smithsonian Guide to Historic America*, Workman Publishing, New York, NY, 1990

Walker, Dale L., *Buckey O'Neill, The Story of a Rough Rider*, The University of Arizona Press, Tucson, AZ, 1970

Weston, James J., *Sharlot Hall: Arizona's Pioneer Lady of Literature*, reprinted from *Journal of the West*, Vol. IV, No. 4, Oct. 1965

MAGAZINES AND ARTICLES

Barks, Cindy, "Prescott cemetery rests in not-so-peaceful setting," *The Prescott Daily Courier*, August 25, 1996

Bates, Al, "The Days of Empire at Prescott's Fort Whipple," *The Prescott Daily Courier*, February 27, 2000
"Clear Pioneer Cemetery Here," Sharlot Hall Museum Archives

Comfort, Charles, "The saga of an astute artist, organizer, raconteur," *The Prescott Daily Courier*, September 13, 1970

Despain, Karen, "Prescott's Silent Citizens: Statues Remember Times of Yesterday," *The Prescott Daily Courier*, February 11, 2000

Gorby, Ricard, "Buckey O'Neill's Advice for Horse Owners," *The Prescott Daily Courier*, February 6, 2000

Ludwig, Charles, "Cowboy With a Brush," *Sunday Digest*, June 28, 1970

Mikulewicz, R.T., "Artist George Phippen Lives Western," *The Prescott Daily Courier*, 1963

Moss, Sandy, "The Arts Dream On: Efforts Pay Off With the Promise of a Bright Future," *The Prescott Daily Courier*, Dec. 30, 1999

Moss, Sandy, "Swept by Fire," *The Prescott Daily Courier*, July 14, 2000

Nordbrock, Anita, and Juti A. Winchester, "Prescott's Extraordinary Women," *The Prescott Daily Courier*, March 5, 2000

Sims, Richard, "Whipping Up a Museum at Old Fort Whipple," *The Prescott Daily Courier*, January 30, 2000

Spano, Susan, "Grand Canyon's Grand Dame," *The Los Angeles Times*, as reprinted in the *Arizona Republic*, December 5, 1999

Tessman, Norm, "Captain William Owen 'Buckey' O'Neill (1860-1898)," Sharlot Hall Museum Archives

"Tribute to Gallant Heroes! Arizona Honors Buckey O'Neill and the Rough Riders," *Arizona Miner*, July 4, 1907, Sharlot Hall Museum Archives

"Who Was Sharlot M. Hall?" Sharlot Hall Museum Archives

BOOKLETS AND PAMPHLETS

Aronowitz, Marguerite Madison (edited by Warren Miller), *The Great Prescott Fire of July 14, 1900*, The Prescott Downtown Partnership, July 2000

Historic Downtown Prescott, Arizona Walking Tour Guide, Prescott Chamber of Commerce

Victorian Homes and Historic Buildings, Prescott Historical Society

THESIS

Yoder, Phillip D., *The History of Fort Whipple*, Master's thesis, University of Arizona Graduate College, Department of History, 1951.

Index

Acknowledgements

The author wishes to thank the artists and their families, especially family members of those artists no longer with us, for their help in compiling the information contained in this book. Also of great assistance were personnel representing the museums, colleges, chambers of commerce, hotels and restaurants, cemeteries, fine art foundries, National Parks and Monuments, and the Prescott Zoo. A special note of appreciation goes to Nancy Burgess of the City of Prescott, Frank Cimorelli of the Northern Arizona VA Healthcare System, Nancy Hayden of the Prescott-Yavapai Native American Indian Tribe, Paul Long of the Smoki Museum, Warren Miller of the Sharlot Hall Museum, Bob Munson of Fort Verde State Historic Park, and Ellen Seeley of Grand Canyon National Park.

Photographs

All photographs, except where noted, were taken by the author. Photographer Pamela DeMarais can be reached at her studio in Minneapolis, Minnesota: pdemarais@stribmail.com.

To order additional copies of this book, send check or money order for $19.95 per book, plus postage and handling, to Pine Castle Books, P.O. Box 4397, Prescott AZ 86302-4397. Arizona residents add sales tax (7.7% or $1.54) per book. Postage and handling: $3.00 for first book, $.75 for each additional book. Please allow 3-4 weeks for delivery.

Marguerite Madison Aronowitz is a professional writer and editor who, along with her husband Fred, live in the Prescott area. While working as a volunteer at the Prescott Visitors Center, she became aware of the need for a comprehensive listing of the many art pieces available to the public that can be found in and around the city. While pursuing information about the beautiful bronze sculptures in Courthouse Plaza, she expanded her search to paintings and museums, and added a listing of historic buildings, Victorian homes and cemeteries. Detailed biographical information on several artists whose work can be found in Prescott and northern Arizona, along with short histories and easy excursions, round out the pages. Marguerite received her B.A. in Communications from the University of Minnesota, and is a member of the Arizona Book Publishing Association. She has previously authored a World War II book entitled, *MATERNITY WARD: Final Flight of a WWII Liberator,* in which she chronicles the life of her cousin in North Africa during the war, and the mission on which he was killed. This ill-fated low-level strike on the oil fields of Ploesti, Romania, took place on August 1, 1943.

294